THE FIRST EPISTLE
TO THE CORINTHIANS

EUGEN WALTER

CROSSROAD · NEW YORK

1981
The Crossroad Publishing Company
575 Lexington Avenue, New York, NY 10022

Originally published as *Der erste Brief an die Korinther*
© 1968 by Patmos-Verlag
from the series *Geistliche Schriftlesung*
edited by Wolfgang Trilling
with Karl Hermann Schelke and Heinz Schürmann

English translation © 1971 by Sheed and Ward, Ltd.
Translated by Simon and Erika Young

Library of Congress Catalog Card Number: 81-68171
ISBN: 0-8245-0122-5

PREFACE

The First Epistle of Paul to the Corinthians is one of the most challenging books for the New Testament interpreter. The reader will be helped by some statement of the challenge and by some assurance that the author of this commentary has met the challenge. First Corinthians is second in length of Paul's epistles after Romans. Unlike Romans, it has almost no structure; it answers successively a number of unrelated questions. In spite of the lack of order and structure, only a little understanding of the questions raised in the epistle is required in order for the reader to see why First Corinthians is one of the most interesting of Paul's epistles.

The secret of the lasting interest of the epistle is that Paul answers each question in depth; and his method of handling the questions deserves close study. The method is rarely used either by preachers, spiritual counselors, or ecclesiastical superiors. Paul fails only when he discusses what women should wear on their heads; on this problem no man has ever spoken with assurance or conviction, and here only Paul interposes brute authority. Possibly his position had more reason in it than we can see, but he himself was aware that his argument was weak. His purpose was not to subdue or to command or to impose his will but to set the mind at rest, to bring the Corinthians to follow his directions because they shared his faith and his understanding. It is an approach so rare that one might think it novel. How successful it was we cannot tell. Paul seems to move at a rather lofty level for those who could not have been Christians for more than five years.

5

It does seem that there is no Christian group so small that it cannot divide into factions. Paul does not attempt to patch up the rents. He asks the Corinthians to contemplate the basis of Christian unity; and this theme recurs throughout the letter, so much so that disunity seems to have been the major problem as Paul saw it. Yet the disunity does not seem to have been deep by our standards, probably no deeper than what we regard as normal disunity in the Christian community. The difference between Paul and us is that this normal disunity was a matter of serious concern to him; it kept the Corinthians from seeing and achieving the vision of Christian unity which he presented to them.

Personal allegiance to different apostles led Paul to consider the apostolic office, and his consideration produced the basic treatise on the Christian ministry. Far from going beyond his treatise, we have usually failed to reach it. The scandal of incest moves Paul to think of sin as the permanent reality of the human condition; grace permits the Christian to live with it and to overcome it, but not by withdrawal from the human race. If one feels no pain when Christians take their differences to civil courts, does this mean that one has fully accepted the principles of Christian tolerance and reconciliation? The problems of marriage are always conditioned by the social structure in which the marriage exists; but one wonders whether the Christian community has ever fully grasped the implications of Paul's statement that " the brother or sister is not enslaved in these circumstances; for God has called you in peace " (7:15). In what circumstances is the brother or sister enslaved? Or when does God not call in peace?

The question of scandal to the weak is treated not only at length, but with digressions, including another discussion of the apostolic office. Possibly there is no more contemporary principle stated in the epistle than the principle that one is not obliged to use all the freedom one has; that the exercise of one's personal freedom without thought may inhibit the personal freedom of another; that one must not make one's own understanding of personal freedom an absolute.

With the Eucharist Paul returns to the theme of Christian unity. Only in very recent years has the eucharistic symbolism of unity been restored to the liturgy; that the symbolism is meaningful is sadly attested by those who find it painful when a unity in which they do not believe is symbolized in liturgical worship. One must remember that this passage of First Corinthians is the earliest theological discussion of the Eucharist in the New Testament; and it is strange to hear some poorly informed modern Catholics say that the eucharistic symbolism of unity is a theological novelty. The practical problems of the gifts of the Spirit are also discussed as a part of liturgical worship; here the symbolism of unity appears in order and decorum in worship.

To many readers Paul's lengthy discussion of the gifts of the Spirit is something of a problem of faith; why do not such gifts appear in the contemporary church? There is indeed something of a problem, but it is too large to be treated here; and Paul himself furnishes the basis for the solution. The greatest of all gifts is love; and it is love, not speaking in tongues or working miracles, which truly and surely attests the presence and working of the Spirit. Paul certainly thought of love as the most wonderful manifestation of the Spirit. Very probably modern Christians rarely think of Christian love as something more marvelous than miracles and tongues. Would Paul suggest that we do not think of it as marvelous because we rarely if ever experience it or feel it? We should indeed have concern about the present working of the Spirit among us, but it is not the absence of miracles and tongues which causes our concern. It is the absence of that love which Paul describes in chapter 13.

Paul's treatment of the resurrection is also the earliest treatment of this topic at length in the New Testament. One knows that the effort of Paul to make the resurrection credible to the Corinthians is directed to others besides the Corinthians. Before Paul no one had spoken in such terms of the potentialities which God has implanted in human existence, and very few after him. Preachers and theologians have rarely been able to match authentic concern for man in this world with genuine faith in eschatological fulfillment as Paul has done. He moves surely between the two extremes of secularism and withdrawal from the world of men. Even on lesser problems he turns the light of the whole Christian perspective. The perspective is so clear that the modern Christian may in its light reach solutions for particular problems other than those reached by Paul; Paul too was conditioned by his society, and he knew it. He is one of the few Christian teachers who was not afraid to deny that for some questions he had no word from the Lord. He did not multiply absolutes. Such totally Christian thinking is hard to achieve. This epistle is an inspiration to strive for it.

JOHN L. McKENZIE

OUTLINE

THE HEADING OF THE LETTER (1 : 1–9)

I. The opening greeting (1 : 1–3)

II. The opening prayer (1 : 4–9)

The Body of the Letter (1 : 10—16 : 18)

AGAINST FACTIONS AND THEIR CAUSES (1 : 10—4 : 21)

I. The four groups in Corinth (1 : 10–17)
   1. Paul sets out the facts (1 : 10–12)
   2. His name has been wrongly identified with a faction (1 : 13–17)

II. The arrogance of Greek culture as the real cause of all factions (1 : 18—2 : 5)
   1. God has saved the world not through " wisdom " but through " folly " (1 : 18–25)
   2. The Corinthian community can perceive this law of grace in its own foundation (1 : 26–31)
   3. Paul himself has consciously based his missionary method on this law of the cross (2 : 1–5)

III. The true supernatural wisdom that is reserved to those advanced in the faith (2 : 6—3 : 4)
   1. There is in Christianity a true wisdom (2 : 6–16)
   2. Unfortunately, the Corinthians are still far removed from this wisdom (3 : 1–4)

IV. Remedies for the Corinthians' factional spirit (3 : 5–23)
   1. The correct attitude towards the church's leaders (3 : 5–9)
   2. The judgment that threatens all who have responsibility for others (3 : 10–17)
   3. The danger that wisdom will turn into folly (3 : 18–23)

9

V. Warnings (4:1–13)
1. Warning against rash judgment upon pastors of souls (4:1–5)
2. Warning against an overestimation of self (4:6–8)
3. In contrast, the Apostle's representation of himself (4:9–13)

VI. The more personal and forgiving tone of this exchange (4:14–21)
1. The Apostle's fatherly love for the community (4:14–16)
2. The mission of the apostolic visitor (4:17)
3. The announcement of his own visit (4:18–21)

ON VARIOUS MORAL ABUSES (5:1—6:20)

I. The case of incest and its purification by the community (5:1–13)
1. The sinner must be excommunicated (5:1–5)
2. The community must preserve its Easter purity and new-ness (5:6–8)
3. The community has the strict obligation to apply ecclesi-astical sanctions against public sinners (5:9–13)

II. Legal proceedings by Christians before pagan courts (6:1–11)
1. Christians should not bring each other before pagan courts (6:1–6)
2. Christians should not go to law at all (6:7–8)
3. Christians must know that they have left the vices of the world behind them (6:9–11)

III. Against lax notions of impurity (6:12–20)
1. The body is more than the stomach (6:12–14)
2. Immorality in the baptized is a profaning of Christ (6:15–17)
3. The body of the baptized man is a temple of the Holy Spirit (6:18–20)

ANSWERS TO VARIOUS QUESTIONS FROM THE COMMUNITY (7:1—14:40)

I. On marriage and virginity (7:1–40)
1. The most important and fundamental clarification, above all concerning marriage (7:1–7)
a) Right and necessity of marriage as the normal condition even of Christians (7:1–2)

b) Man and wife have the same rights and the same duties in marriage (7:3–4)
c) Temporary continence is to be recommended for spiritual reasons (7:5)
d) Marriage and virginity: two gifts of grace (7:6–7)
2. Consequences for particular marriage cases (7:8–16)
    a) Freedom to marry, commitment in marriage (7:8–11)
    b) Two different possibilities for marriage in which one party remains an unbeliever (*Privilegium Paulinum*) (7:12–16)
3. Vocation and profession: On the relation of Christianity to the secular order (7:17–24)
    a) The example of circumcision: a contribution on the problem of the Jews (7:17–19)
    b) The example of slavery: a contribution on the social question (7:20–24)
4. Clarifications concerning voluntary celibacy (7:25–35)
    a) Recommendation of celibacy (7:25–28)
    b) The spirit of detachment or virginity required of all (7:29–31)
    c) Where the advantage of the virgin state lies (7:32–35)
5. Final detailed advice for two special groups (7:36–40)
    a) To fathers of grown-up daughters (7:36–38)
    b) To widows (7:39–40)

II. On freedom and its proper use (8:1—11:1)
1. Practical difficulties in the use of food offered to idols (8:1–13)
    a) What must be the touchstone: knowledge or love? (8:1–3)
    b) What knowledge knows and does not know (8:4–6)
    c) What love does (8:7–13)
2. The example of the Apostle in limiting his own freedom (9:1–27)
    a) The Corinthians seem to have understood the Apostle's conduct badly, or even to have misunderstood it altogether (9:1–6)
    b) The rights of an Apostle correspond to a general human and even divine law (9:7–10)
    c) They are completely appropriate to the spiritual field (9:11–14)

   d) Nevertheless, Paul has made no use of them (9:15–18)
   e) . . . In the first place for pastoral reasons (9:19–22)
   f) . . . But also so as not to risk his own salvation (9:23–27)

   3. Warning examples from the history of Israel of a false
      assurance of salvation (10:1–13)
      a) The sacraments do not guarantee salvation . . . (10:1–5)
      b) . . . For those who challenge the Lord (10:6–11)
      c) But God is faithful to those who truly hope in him
         (10:12–13)

   4. Practical decisions on the question of food offered in sacri-
      fice (10:14—11:1)
      a) Either: participation in the body of Christ (10:14–17)
      b) Or: Partnership with Demons (10:18–22)
      c) What can be said in private cases (10:23–30)
      d) What applies to all cases and in the last analysis
         (10:31—11:1)

III. On conduct in the liturgical assembly (11:2–34)
   1. The veiling of women in the communal assembly (11:2–16)
      a) The more general theological and human arguments
         (11:2–6)
      b) Biblical considerations (11:7–12)
      c) The appeal to natural sensibility (11:13–15)
      d) Regard for Church tradition (11:16)

   2. The proper celebration of the Lord's supper (11:17–34)
      a) The abuses that have arisen (11:17–22)
      b) The establishment of the Lord's supper as the source
         and norm for the community celebration (11:23–25)
      c) The moral consequences that follow from this (11:26–29)
      d) The consequences of disregard (11:30–32)
      e) Immediate practical injunction (11:33–34)

IV. The significance of charisms for the church (12:1—14:40)
   1. The variety of spiritual gifts in the Church (12:1–31)
      a) The man who speaks with God's spirit is recognized
         first and foremost by his profession of Jesus (12:1–3)
      b) The gifts of the Spirit are many, the Spirit himself is one
         and the same (12:4–11)
      c) Analogy of the body and its members (12:12–26)
      d) Its application to the body of Christ (12:27–31)

2. The highest of all gifts and most important of all virtues: love (13:1–13)
   a) Without love all things, even the best, are nothing (13:1–3)
   b) Love itself brings forth all that is good in superabundance (13:4–7)
   c) Only love is already now what it can be for eternity (13:8–13)
3. Directions appropriate to all the circumstances concerning the spiritual gifts of speaking in tongues and of prophesying (14:1–40)
   a) Why prophecy deserves to take precedence over speaking in tongues (14:1–25)
   b) Practical consequences (14:26–40)

THE RESURRECTION OF THE BODY (15:1–58)
   I. Christ's rising: the basis and center of the gospel (15:1–11)
      1. All Christian preaching rests on the apostolic tradition (15:1–3a)
      2. The apostolic tradition rests on the official list of witnesses of the Resurrection (15:3b–8)
      3. The list of witnesses is completed by Paul (15:9–11)
   II. Our resurrection stands and falls with the Resurrection of Christ (15:12–19)
      1. The Resurrection is indivisible (15:12–13)
      2. Our faith stands and falls with Christ's Resurrection (15:14–16)
      3. Our entire hope rests on Christ's Resurrection (15:17–19)
   III. The totality of the Resurrection seen in the light of saving history (15:20–28)
      1. The principle of Resurrection (15:20–22)
      2. The stages of Resurrection (15:23–24)
      3. The final completion (15:25–28)
   IV. Human considerations (15:29–34)
      1. The " baptism on behalf of the dead " (15:29)
      2. The Apostle's life expounded (15:30–32a)
      3. A collection of pressing motives and palpable warnings (15:32b–34)

V. The nature of the risen body (15 : 35 -44a)
   1. Illustrated by the analogy of the transformation of seedcorn
      (15 : 35–38)
   2. Expounded by comparison with the many forms and levels
      of life and living bodies (15 : 39–41)
   3. Celebrated in a short antiphonal hymn (15 : 42–44a)

VI. A survey from the last things to the first, and the first things to
    the last (15 : 44b–58)
   1. The first Adam and the last (15 : 44b–49)
   2. The all-embracing transformation (15 : 50–53)
   3. The expected song of victory (15 : 54–57)
   4. The present consolation (15 : 58)

OFFICIAL AND PERSONAL MATTERS : INSIGHTS INTO THE BEGINNINGS OF
   THE WORLD-WIDE LIFE OF THE PRIMITIVE CHURCH (16 : 1–18)
   I. The levy for Jerusalem (16 : 1–4)

  II. The Apostle's Immediate Travel Plans (16 : 5–9)

 III. The journey of the two apostolic representatives (16 : 10–12)

 IV. Final injunctions (16 : 13–18)

THE ENDING OF THE LETTER (16 : 19–24)

THE HEADING OF THE LETTER
(1:1–9)

The Opening Greeting (1:1–3)

In antiquity every letter had three starting points: the sender, the recipient, and the greeting. Paul had no reason to depart from this custom, even though his letter was not intended as a private document but as a " pastoral letter," a message to a community issued in God-given authority and responsibility. From the combination of these two elements there arises a very individual style in which one perceives both what is quite personal and what is official. Three phrases would have sufficed: Paul—to the Corinthians—greetings. What a transformation of this skeleton occurs under the inspiration of the new spirit, the Holy Spirit! What richness is gathered together and revealed in these three starting points.

¹Paul, called by the will of God to be an apostle of Christ Jesus, and our brother Sosthenes, ²to the church of God which is at Corinth, to those sanctified in Christ Jesus, called to be saints together with all those who in every place call on the name of our Lord Jesus Christ, both their Lord and ours: ³Grace to you and peace from God our Father and the Lord Jesus Christ.

The facts the Apostle links to his name are an immediate and forcible reminder that for Christians he is not just anyone. In the title Apostle, become all too familiar and colorless to us, we have to understand the original meaning of a fully authorized ambassador. This should not be seen only in the juridical sense of plenipotentiary, for according to the view current at the time of Jesus, the emissary was equivalent to the sender himself. Paul strengthens the official role still further by two additions: he is called by " the will of God." Without doubt he is bringing into play here the event at Damascus, but in such a way that behind Christ, who appeared to him there in visible form, God himself can be seen as the ultimate summoner. This is how Paul, fundamentally, understands Christ: what becomes visible in him is the invisible God, exactly as Christ proclaimed in the Gospel of John: " He who has seen me has seen the Father " (Jn. 14:9).

Paul names, in addition to himself, " our brother Sosthenes." To name a co-apostle or co-worker corresponds not only to a literary habit of his but also to the practice of the early Church of always sending out two missionaries together (e.g. Barnabas and Paul, Acts 13:2). Reference can also be made to Jesus' own sending (Lk. 10:1).

The recipients we call simply the Corinthians. How much fuller and more honorable is the address in the Apostle's mouth: " To the church of God which is at Corinth." Certainly the word *ekklesia*—Church—was already known in Corinth. In all Greek democracies this was the name of the assembly of enfranchised citizens in a city. When Paul addresses this assembly, this community, as the " *ekklesia* of God," he makes it clear that it has been summoned and has gathered together in God's name. The verbal association of the " call " is therefore once again taken up by him and made his own. Holiness, as he emphasizes again later on, comes from the God who is sending forth his call in this neighborhood. For the man who knows how to listen, all this is already contained in the genitive formation " church of God." To an ear attuned to and taught by the Old Testament, this expression has already been coined there to mean the community of God's people assembled for the sacred liturgy. Paul, by writing to Corinth in this way, is thereby saying in an all-embracing way that God is now everywhere making ready for himself his chosen people, that the old privileges are being extended. Yes, extended, because it still remains the one holy community of God, even though it is no longer possible for all to gather together in one place, since its members are soon to be spread out over the whole of society as the *catholica ecclesia*.

The words " together with all those who in every place call on the name of our Lord Jesus Christ " signify a remarkable broadening of the horizon. We discover that there are Christians in the surrounding region between Ephesus and Corinth, or even farther afield. The Apostle immediately takes the occasion to bring it home to his Corinthians that they are not alone in being the church of " their Lord and ours." To " call on the name of our Lord Jesus Christ, both their lord and ours " is the simple duty of a Christian. It is the continuation of the Old Testament expression to " call on the name of Yahweh." For this reason the Greek translation, which Paul used throughout, always spoke of calling on the name of the Lord. Paul always thought it right to apply God's title of " Lord " to Christ. In both Old and New Testament this use of the Lord's name in calling upon him serves to make a distinction and separation from any kind of worship or invocation of pagan gods. The man who calls on the name of the Lord Jesus Christ is a member of the Church wherever he is, even if he is lonely and forsaken in his district or his house.

The Apostle's greeting becomes a blessing, the conferring by the power of God of good things that men can otherwise only wish for one another.

The Opening Prayer (1:4-9)

The Apostle follows the good epistolary custom which applied in antiquity as it still does today of not beginning with unpleasant things (of which there will be a few in this letter), but with something friendly to think about or be thankful for. Paul, of course, is not content with human praise or with recognition of what is praiseworthy, but with thanksgiving to God. If we consider the matter properly, we find ourselves being witnesses here to St. Paul's personal prayer.

[4]I give thanks to God always for you because of the grace of God which was given you in Christ Jesus, [5]that in every way you were enriched in him with all speech and all knowledge—[6]even as the testimony to Christ was confirmed among you—[7]so that you are not lacking in any spiritual gift, as you wait for the revealing of our Lord Jesus Christ; [8]who will sustain you to the end, guiltless in the day of our Lord Jesus Christ. [9]God is faithful, by whom you were called into the fellowship of his Son, Jesus Christ our Lord.

When Paul thanks God for his grace, this expression includes the entire scheme of salvation that is contained in Christ. We cannot but be amazed at what he draws out of this treasury. For whereas elsewhere at the start of his letters he speaks of faith, hope, and love as the foundation and basic acts and powers of the Christian life (cf. 1 Thess. 1 : 3), here Paul speaks of " speech and knowledge." What is meant, its real and supposed value, will occupy us for several chapters. But it would be as well to listen carefully from the start.

The establishment or reinforcement of the witness to Christ

can be understood in two ways—as the inner securing of the
Corinthians' faith, or as the outward confirmation of the apostolic preaching by means of miracles, which often accompanied
the Apostle's preaching (cf. also 2 : 4), as Jesus had foretold (Mk.
16 : 7f.).

After the Apostle has once again acknowledged the treasury
of grace—this time under the title of " charisma," the word
which was to receive so special a meaning from this very letter
—he, the man of prayer, who is here also the leader in prayer,
draws the attention of his companions in prayer to the day when
all that is now of grace will be made fully manifest.

THE BODY OF THE LETTER
(1:10—16:18)

AGAINST FACTIONS AND THEIR CAUSES
(1:10—4:21)

The Four Groups in Corinth (1:10–17)

The first great theme of the letter extends over four entire chapters: the prevailing division of the community at Corinth into groups or cliques. Positively expressed, it is the theme of the unity of the Church. First, Paul sets out the facts in all openness (1 : 10–12). Then it appears as though he is about to go into the question of principle involved (1 : 13), but first he allows himself a personal observation (1 : 14–17) which, in its final sentence, gives him the opportunity to uncover the deepest source of the evil.

Paul Sets Out the Facts (1 :10–12)

[10]*I appeal to you, brethren, by the name of our Lord Jesus Christ, that all of you agree and that there be no dissensions among you, but that you be united in the same mind and the same judgment.* [11]*For it has been reported to me by Chloe's people that there is quarreling among you, my brethren.* [12]*What I mean is that each one of you says, " I belong to Paul," or " I belong to Apollos," or " I belong to Cephas," or " I belong to Christ."*

It is with an appeal that the Apostle usually opens the second, practical, pastoral part of his great epistles. Here he goes at once to the subject that he perhaps saw as the most important. But

23

before he brings up the painful subject, the Apostle gives two further, interconnected indications of the level at which, and the atmosphere in which, he wishes to be heard. He speaks to " brethren " and " by the name of Our Lord Jesus Christ." Only an appeal coming from Jesus Christ, our divine Lord and brother, can be so loving and persuasive, so commanding and yet sympathetic. Those he has drawn to himself he has also brought together among themselves in a new way. He has given them a new feeling for life, and this enables them to recognize each other as brothers.

When the situation has been described, Paul names the source from which he knows of it. A woman who was reliable and who acted with true responsibility informed the Apostle through her people—relatives or perhaps employees in her business. It is important that Paul is not dependent on anonymous letters, and the name of this woman, Chloe, gives an interesting example of how, in the young Church, women could certainly have respect, judgment, influence and a voice.

The danger of a break up of the community had certainly been recognized at an early stage. Enough of it had appeared to create a lasting vigilance lest the personal style of the leaders, in particular the preference for one or other of them, should damage the unity and singlemindedness of the community.

His Name Has Been Wrongly Identified with a Faction (*1:13-17*)

[13]*Is Christ divided? Was Paul crucified for you? Or were you baptized in the name of Paul?* [14]*I am thankful that I baptized none of you except Crispus and Gaius;* [15]*lest anyone should say that you were baptized in my name.* [16]*(I did baptize also the*

household of Stephanas. Beyond that, I do not know whether I
baptized anyone else.) [17]*For Christ did not send me to baptize*
but to preach the gospel, and not with eloquent wisdom, lest the
cross of Christ be emptied of its power.

Paul fixes on the last-named faction, those who misused the name
of Christ, to show to all the evil and folly of such divisions. For
it is not possible to set one over against the other at the same
level—Christ and Paul (or Apollos or Cephas). Whoever destroys
unity rends Christ asunder. Here it becomes apparent for an
instant how deeply Paul envisages the unity between Christ and
the Church (the community). The two ironical questions referring to Paul are very tactfully chosen, inasmuch as Paul does not
attack directly the other two around whose persons or names
parties had formed. He dares to hope that people will not fail to
apply his remarks equally to themselves. In any case no one was
to think that Paul was fighting for his own position in the community. We can also learn from the way the two questions
parallel each other how Christ's crucifixion and the baptism of
Christians belong most closely together, a point more precisely
expounded in Romans 6:3ff. And it is precisely because these
two belong so closely together that no third party can intervene to
play a separate role, that of " baptizer." On the other hand, it is
not far-fetched to hold that the administration of baptism creates
a special link between the minister and the baptized person. This
opinion is not to be unconditionally condemned or rejected. All
the more painful is it when Paul expresses a sense of separation
by actually thanking God that there is no one in Corinth whom
he has baptized. But leaving aside the polemical emphasis, it
may be thought surprising that Paul baptized so little, and that
on principle.

In the second half of the sentence Paul moves over to an analysis that illuminates the ultimate relations of salvation and perdition in the light of the Corinthian factions. The important aspects of this at first surprising observation are enlarged on in the next section.

The Arrogance of Greek Culture as the Real Cause of All Factions (1:18—2:5)

With the catchword " *sophia*," wisdom, Paul takes up a favorite expression of the Hellenistic culture at that time. *Sophia* had become the very measure of the Greek evaluation of men and ideas. If we translate it as " wisdom," we strike not far from a similar nerve in our own self-understanding today. The Apostle, in an ever-mounting paradox, opposes to this *sophia* the folly and weakness of the cross as God's wisdom and God's power (1 : 18–25). Then he draws the Corinthians' attention to their own community so that they can see this same law of grace confirmed in its formation (1 : 26–31). To this proof from experience he adds another, by referring to the manner of his own first appearance and activity which led to the foundation of the community (2 : 1–5). All this shows that God does not set store by what appears as human wisdom but rather by the making visible of grace that exceeds all human possibility.

God Has Saved the World Not through "Wisdom" but through "Folly" (1:18-25)

18*For the word of the cross is folly to those who are perishing,* *but to us who are being saved it is the power of God. ¹⁹For it is written,*

" I will destroy the wisdom of the wise,
and the cleverness of the clever I will thwart."

²⁰*Where is the wise man? Where is the scribe? Where is the debater of this age? Has not God made foolish the wisdom of the world? ²¹For since, in the wisdom of God, the world did not know God through wisdom, it pleased God through the folly of what we preach to save those who believe.*

The Apostle's brief reference in the preceding verse to his manner of preaching—he is to come back to it at greater length (2 : 1–5) —served to set out formally his first great theme, positive and negative, challenging, indeed shocking, yet no more violently challenging or shocking than was and remains for all time the cross of God's son. Let each man see to what this cross challenges him, for upon it depends eternal salvation or perdition.

" The wise man, the scribe, the debater "—it is difficult to make out whether Paul means, in using these three expressions, to refer to Jewish as well as Greek conditions. But it is certain that on the whole he intends to draw together and cover both here—everything that rests only on human capacity, humanistic values, and natural powers. Creation contains so much matter for inexhaustible wonder at God's wisdom that man can find God's glory in it (Rom. 1 : 19ff.).

²²*For Jews demand signs and Greeks seek wisdom, ²³but we preach Christ crucified, a stumbling block to Jews and folly to Gentiles, ²⁴but to those who are called, both Jews and Greeks, Christ the power of God and the wisdom of God. ²⁵For the fool-*

*ishness of God is wiser than men, and the weakness of God is
stronger than men.*

" For Jews demand signs and Greeks seek wisdom." There
could be no briefer and more telling way of summing up the
difference between two basically diverse mentalities. In this
double characterization the grandeur and dangers of the Israel-
ite and the Hellenistic spirit are recognized: the religion of the
prophets on the one hand; the culture of the philosophers on the
other. It is frightening that it is sometimes the best that bars the
way to the faith which alone brings blessedness. But had not God
himself always pointed out his messengers by means of signs?
Was not the whole of saving history, the way of salvation on
which God guided the people of his covenant, marked by signs
—the way out of Egypt to Sinai, and from Sinai through the
desert to the promised land? Was it not to be expected that he
would also proclaim by signs the new and final salvation? But
Jesus had already held it against the Pharisees and scribes that
" an evil and adulterous generation seeks for a sign; but no sign
shall be given to it except the sign of the prophet Jonah " (Mt.
12:38f.). Man is always inclined to take so tight a hold on what
is granted him that he rejects any alternatives.

*The Corinthian Community Can Perceive This Law of Grace in Its
Own Foundation (1:26–31)*

*²⁶For consider your call, brethren; not many of you were wise
according to worldly standards, not many were powerful, not
many were of noble birth; ²⁷but God chose what is foolish in the
world to shame the wise, God chose what is weak in the world*

to shame the strong, [28]God chose what is low and despised in the world, even things that are not, to bring to nothing things that are, [29]so that no human being might boast in the presence of God. [30]He is the source of your life in Christ Jesus, whom God made our wisdom, our righteousness and sanctification and redemption; [31]therefore, as it is written, " Let him who boasts, boast of the Lord."

Paul has given the community an insight into the depths of the divine way to salvation and into its world-wide extent. Suddenly he introduces a completely new and personal element by drawing attention to the spectators themselves—does not what has happened to them through God's summons follow the same pattern? The majority of the community have not come from the upper layers of the intelligentsia, of wealth, or of nobility. There are more small shopkeepers, manual workers, and dockers than professors, presidents of banks, and shipowners. On the other hand, it is also interesting for us to note that such people were not totally lacking. A wealth of intellect or possessions need not be an obstacle to faith and grace while, conversely, not every poor man is receptive to the riches of God.

Paul Himself Has Consciously Based His Missionary Method on This Law of the Cross (2:1–5)

[1]*When I came to you, brethren, I did not come proclaiming to you the testimony of God in lofty words or wisdom. [2]For I decided to know nothing among you except Jesus Christ and him crucified. [3]And I was with you in weakness and in much fear and trembling; [4]and my speech and my message were not*

in plausible words of wisdom, but in demonstration of the Spirit and power, ⁵that your faith might not rest in the wisdom of men but in the power of God.

The Corinthians can of course seek the law of grace illustrated in themselves, that is, in the foundation of their community, which ran contrary to all human expectations and values. But the Apostle's first activity in Corinth also offers them an excellent illustration of it if they will recall it now. When they came to the faith through him, they were perhaps not consciously aware of it. Enlightened by faith, they were able to penetrate to the wonder of the message of salvation of the crucified Son of God. But when he brings those weeks to their minds, they will have to agree that his appearance, his preaching, and his whole manner were anything but impressive or overpowering. He makes it deeply evident that God has encouraged him with an extraordinary gift of consolation. The description in Acts 18:9 recalls Jesus' experience on the Mount of Olives and also certain experiences of the prophets. Here too is found the Old Testament expression " fear and trembling."

Paul affirms this with a full heart. The messenger of him who redeemed us on the cross must give up his own life also. Why? Paul puts forward only one reason here: in order that the faith of those he wins by his preaching should not mistakenly be confined to him, whether because of his impressive personality or because of his compelling presentation. The personality of the messenger is indeed drawn into the message, thus making it effective, but not by a kind of reduction by this man and his human wisdom to the level of a purely human conviction, but in a deeper relationship. The mystery of the cross is repeated in its servants and takes in their entire existence. If he has thereby also pointed to the meaning of " spirit," this was not the human spirit, however impressive, but *pneuma*, the supernatural power of God. The two expressions " spirit and power " belong so closely to each other that they almost mean the same thing, and in any case mutually illustrate each other. *Pneuma* here is God's power, and this power comes in the Spirit. In itself this could certainly refer to miracles, which often accompanied the Apostles' work, as is reported also of this missionary journey (Acts 16: 16–26). But it could also mean the more spiritual miracles of conversion, and in the context as a whole this is more likely for Corinth. That people open their hearts to this message with all its consequences is basically always a miracle.

The True Supernatural Wisdom that Is Reserved to Those Advanced in the Faith (2:6—3:4)

The desire for a higher knowledge and a deeper insight is not in itself reprehensible. It is awakened by God himself. If the urge to growth even among the lowest forms of life springs from God, should not the human spirit, destined of its nature for eternity, strive for ever greater fulfillment and completion? " Wisdom " is in itself not a bad title for this objective. In the saving history of the Old Testament there is even a whole phase that is known by it. From it come the " Books of Wisdom." But just as these have as their implicit basis God's revelation to Moses and the prophets, and indeed at bottom consist of nothing other than an ever renewed investigation and exploration of this revelation, and its confrontation with all kinds of human experience, so too a Christian wisdom can only exist on the basis of faith which, in the first instance, demands the renunciation of any wisdom of one's own. After the Apostle has explained this divine wisdom as imparted to the mature (2:6–9), he shows its connection with the gifts of the Spirit (2:10–16).

There Is in Christianity a True Wisdom (2:6–16)

[6]*Yet among the mature we do impart wisdom, although it is not a wisdom of this age or of the rulers of this age, who are doomed to pass away.* [7]*But we impart a secret and hidden wisdom of God, which God decreed before the ages for our glorification.* [8]*None of the rulers of this age understood this; for if they had, they would not have crucified the Lord of glory.* [9]*But, as it is written,*

" What no eye has seen, nor ear heard,
nor the heart of man conceived,
what God has prepared for those who love him," . . .

What wisdom is supposed to make known it seems at once to cover up again, for it is " a secret and hidden wisdom." Both belong to the essence of what Paul means by mystery. It goes quite beyond human understanding, and yet a man can understand this much of it, that it is not totally incomprehensible but only exceeds his own powers of comprehension. It is, however, possible to discover more exactly in what area lies this enlargement of the dimensions of life into eternity. When Paul tells of how this wisdom, or rather what God allows man to know of it, was hidden until now, but from the beginning the revelation of these things was planned for a particular moment and foreseen, and this ordering of salvation aims at our glorification, our participation in God's glory, he thereby defines divine wisdom as totally within the context of saving history, in contrast to all pagan forms of human wisdom, which claim to unveil the

Beyond. It is the measure of the inexpressible value of what is taking place in the presence of saving history—within which Paul and we belong quite closely together!—that it can only be correctly understood in relation to this origin transcending all time past, and to this future reaching out beyond all time to come. It is possible, however, to speak of it now, in the present in which Paul and we ourselves belong together. No wonder that all human speech concerning it can be but a stammer which means nothing to those not initiated into this realm, but makes hearts beat faster among those who are " mature," as Paul puts it to the Corinthians.

" What no eye has seen . . .": this oft-quoted verse is cited by Paul also. But it does not come exactly in this form from any of the canonical books of the Old Testament. It is presumed that it comes from an apocryphal apocalypse of Elijah, but the point can be almost as well taken from Isaiah 64 : 4 : " From of old no one has heard or perceived by the ear, no eye has seen a God besides thee, who works for those who wait for him." This verse is most often taken to refer to the future happiness of heaven, but it seems here to be applied to the present state of Christians, those Christians who possess knowledge of the true wisdom.

[10] . . . *God has revealed to us through the Spirit. For the Spirit searches everything, even the depths of God.* [11]*For what person knows a man's thoughts except the spirit of the man which is in him? So also no one comprehends the thoughts of God except the Spirit of God.* [12]*Now we have received not the spirit of the world, but the Spirit which is from God, that we might understand the gifts bestowed on us by God.*

Who are the " us " to whom, as Paul so emphatically declares,

" God has revealed " ? He has said so many and such lofty things about the state of the baptized (1 : 4–7, 26–31), that one might reply—all who have received the Spirit in baptism. On the other hand, he has also indicated (2 : 6) that there is something reserved to the " mature," and seems subsequently (3 : 1) to deny to the Corinthians the presuppositions for this. The uncertainty and even apparent contradiction can be resolved by an observation that is repeatedly confirmed in Paul's writings. His first person plural is for the most part open-ended. It embraces in principle all the baptized, even if they are in practice not, or not yet, or no longer, included. The man who, in becoming a Christian, has received the Spirit has in principle also received this revelation, the self-communication of God. But it is different when we are dealing with graces which only come to flower and fruition among those who live according to the Spirit, who live a spiritual life in the sense that they cultivate an intercourse with God, love prayer and absorption in scripture, and thus look at the whole world in God's light.

" That we might understand the gifts bestowed on us by God "—we could also say *understand what we are in grace*. Grace belongs to the essence of things and therefore reaches deeper down into the roots of our being than knowledge. That is why a child can already be baptized. In every man who receives grace, this grace is more than he can understand. On the other hand, it is of the nature of grace, which is a participation in God's life and love, that the man who receives it knows that he is continually transcending his own powers because only then does he finally become what he truly *is*. God's joy consists in the fact that his self-knowledge and his being are clothed in eternity. And grace consists in the fact that in eternity man can become like God.

[13]*And we impart this in words not taught by human wisdom but taught by the Spirit, interpreting spiritual truths to those who possess the Spirit. [14]The unspiritual man does not receive the gifts of the Spirit of God, for they are folly to him, and he is not able to understand them because they are spiritually discerned. [15]The spiritual man judges all things, but is himself to be judged by no one. [16]" For who has known the mind of the Lord so as to instruct him? " But we have the mind of Christ.*

The foregoing is said of matters that are, in principle, the concern of everyone initiated into the mystery of Christ. These matters require, however, an appropriate style of speech, at any rate for those who, like Paul, are charged with the ministry of the word. With this he comes to a point that he has already touched on several times. At the very beginning (1:5) he had noted it with appreciation among the Corinthians, but on a later occasion (2:1, 4) he also indicated his reservations. Human speech is necessary for the communication of divine things among men, but this brings with it the danger that the divine message will be judged according to the arts of human speech. Many of the Corinthians did this. Augustine also for a time undervalued the scriptures according to these standards until he realized that this form of speech was much better suited than any poetic work of art to the saving humility of God. One cannot manufacture an appropriate form of speech for this proclamation as though preaching were some kind of technique. One must be a spiritual man in order to be able to speak in the spirit. One must also be a spiritual man in order to be able to hear in the spirit. The language of the spirit thus comes about in a circular way. To receive the spirit, one must first hear the message; but to grasp the message, one must already have the spirit.

The last three words of verse 13 can be translated in very different ways to mean that we interpret spiritual truths to spiritual men or that we interpret spiritual truths with spiritual words. The first rendering follows better from the preceding line of thought, but the second makes a better introduction to the succeeding passage. Objectively it makes hardly any difference. Paul has to tell the Corinthians that they are unspiritual men and therefore set too much store by fine words.

In verse 13 Paul has spoken unmistakably about himself and about his own style of preaching as opposed to that other style by which the Corinthians allowed themselves to be all too greatly impressed. Now he speaks more explicitly from the other point of view, that of acceptance and understanding. He speaks bluntly to these people. But he still expresses himself carefully and tactfully, putting the point in quite general terms and thus leaving it open as to how far it applies to the individual. In opposing the " unspiritual man " to the " spiritual man " he is using a distinction by no means unknown to the Corinthians from contemporary mysticism. The unspiritual man is the man who possesses all the natural and normal capacities of an ordinary man through his soul, his natural spirit, but no more, so long as he is not initiated into the world of God through participation in God's own spirit and thus in God's way of thinking and loving. This natural unspiritual man easily imagines that he can judge everything, precisely because he does not know his limits. He thinks that the spiritual man understands nothing of life, or else he would behave the same as himself. In reality the spiritual man sees much further than the unspiritual, and can judge him, while the opposite is not possible.

With apparent inconsequence Paul closes with an Old Testament saying that at first seems to rule out for men all that he has just proclaimed, only in order to use this saying as the introduction to a most bold application. To the question " who " which seems to allow of no answer, he answers with a " we " triumphant in Christ. We have this " mind " since we have the spirit of Christ. For Paul, the *kyrios* of the Old Testament is always Christ. This is justified because the God of the Old Testament has revealed and communicated himself to us in Christ.

Unfortunately, the Corinthians Are Still Far Removed from This Wisdom (3:1–4)

¹But I, brethren, could not address you as spiritual men, but as men of the flesh, as babes in Christ. ²I fed you with milk, not solid food; for you were not ready for it; and even yet you are not ready, ³for you are still of the flesh. For while there is jealousy and strife among you, are you not of the flesh, and behaving like ordinary men? ⁴For, when one says, " I belong to Paul," and another, " I belong to Apollos," are you not merely men?

Paul delivers this rebuke: If at that time his preaching did not yet reach the heights of Christian wisdom, then the fault was and continued to be theirs. For are not such jealousies, such emphasis on earthly realities to the dangers of the most essential realities of salvation in Christ, proof of how deeply they were still involved at the human, all too human level?

" Are you not merely men? " That is the whole trouble—but it is no excuse for a community of God in Christ Jesus. If they are healed by the Spirit, then they are raised up above the merely human level, and are empowered to see what is human in their pastors as God sees it. Moreover, it is their duty to do so. They commit sin if they draw back from a God-given humanity into a corrupt, natural humanity. Thus evil first comes about which then at once becomes powerful among them.

Remedies for the Corinthians' Factional Spirit (3:5-23)

The interlude concerning the higher wisdom which exists in Christ through the Holy Spirit, but which the Corinthians erroneously thought lacking in the Apostle, has supplied a good preparation for the purging of party division in the community. Now the Apostle goes right to the kernel of the matter, leaving every personal element far behind him. One must admire the skill with which the sting is removed from what is personal here, so that everything is depicted in the light of the Spirit, from above. Here standards are established for all time by which communities have to judge their leaders, and these themselves, in order not to destroy what must be built up. In a rapid succession there is depicted the relative importance of men who are something, and yet are almost nothing in God's saving work—first by images (planting, watering) and then without images (servants, fellow workers).

The Correct Attitude towards the Church's Leaders (3:5-9)

⁵What then is Apollos? What is Paul? Servants through whom you believed, as the Lord assigned to each. ⁶I planted, Apollos watered, but God gave the growth. ⁷So neither he who plants nor he who waters is anything, but only God who gives the growth.

*⁸He who plants and he who waters are equal, and each shall
receive his wages according to his labor. ⁹For we are God's fellow
workers; you are God's field, God's building.*

Of the four parties that have been named at the beginning, Paul
now picks out only two names. It seems in any case as if right
from the start he directed the spearhead of his polemic especially
against the Apollos faction (1 : 18ff.; 2 : 1ff.). It was indeed the
most dangerous, because it exploited the weak point of most
Corinthians. Thus it had now once more to be discussed explicitly
and by name, in order to apply the remedy direct to the wound.
How should one not be able to speak about it quite calmly? To
some Paul was everything. They clung with all their heart to
him who had brought them the good news and grace, but too
easily felt it to be ingratitude and disloyalty if not all took this
attitude. To others the brilliance of the Christian light was first
made apparent by the work of the learned and skillful Apollos.
If the earliest devout soul perhaps spoke always of " Paul," those
others might be tempted to say " that was nothing to Apollos "—
the way children can quarrel and vie with each other. Into this
situation there now comes a word of explanation : Both are servants of your salvation, and each in the way the Lord gives him.
Servants are not those to whom one belongs but those whose
service one gratefully accepts. There are many servants, but there
is only one to whom one can belong—the Lord. If one style
pleases me more or is of more value to me than another, this too
goes back to the Lord who gave it. No one can choose his style.
It is possible that Paul himself sometimes had to comfort himself
with such thought when he found that his style did not everywhere bring a response.

The general picture of " servants " is then made more concrete, more colorful, and more detailed. In each verse new light is thrown on the relationship of the two servants: now positive—planting, watering; now negative—neither is anything without God's blessing; now brought together—both are one in being nothing before God; now distinct—each receives his own particular wages. What really distinguishes them only God can judge. How foolish, therefore, to play them off against each other, as the Corinthians were doing. If to one is granted much success with little effort, while the other strives desperately with small success, because success only comes later to the advantage of others, God will judge and reward all this aright.

In conclusion comes the humble yet proud self-description of all true pastors of souls, " God's fellow workers." The expression " fellow worker " is now much used in the Church and outside as well, but " God's fellow workers " is something quite different. It is completed by what is said of the community; it is God's precious field and his building. This last image leads us into the next section. The two illustrations of planting and building often lead into each other in Paul. Because what is being considered here is the proper estimation of the pastor at work in the community, the community appears, in this image, as only passive. Otherwise it is often enough said that there is no purely passive membership, but that all have to build together.

The Judgment that Threatens All Who Have Responsibility for Others (3:10–17)

[10]*According to the commission of God given to me, like a skilled master builder I laid a foundation, and another man is building upon it. Let each man take care how he builds upon it.* [11]*For no*

*other foundation can anyone lay than that which is laid, which
is Jesus Christ. [12]Now if anyone builds on the foundation with
gold, silver, precious stones, wood, hay, stubble—[13]each man's
work will become manifest; for the Day will disclose it, because
it will be revealed with fire, and the fire will test what sort of
work each one has done. [14]If the work which any man has built
on the foundation survives, he will receive a reward. [15]If any
man's work is burned up, he will suffer loss, though he himself
will be saved, but only as through fire.*

To the townsman Paul, the images of house building meant
more, fundamentally, than those of horticulture or agriculture.
In any case, he can draw points from the building image that are
on the one hand much more personal, apposite, and relevant, and
on the other also much more far-reaching, because they extend to
the final clarification of the last judgment. Paul is conscious that
his apostolic founding of the community happened so totally
according to the mind of God and with God's grace that nothing
can shake this foundation. All the more will the preachers and
pastors who care and will care for the community after him look
to it as the way they can carry this building further. After the
manner of Jesus' parables, Paul suggests two extreme possibilities
in the two groups of building materials, each composed of three
kinds. Only " wood," " hay," and " stubble " were actually real
building materials. With these the poor built their mudhuts, then
as now, around the great cities. " Gold," " silver," and " precious
stones " were used by the rich to decorate their houses. Paul
means to say that just as one can quickly produce a house out of
wood, hay, and stubble, and with clever decoration make people
forget of what cheap material it is made, so too pastors of souls
may have conspicuous successes in their communities. And this

may all continue very satisfactorily as long as there is no fire. But fire *will* strike this building as surely as that Day will come on which all will be revealed. Woe then to those builders. They will indeed escape with their lives, but as someone who has only saved his bare life from the fire. The other half of the image, building with gold, silver, and precious stones, is not developed. For Paul must disillusion those who had fallen for the intellectual, impressive style of Apollos, or had evaluated it one-sidedly. Paul does not say that Apollos has built like this. At least one does not have to interpret it that way. By wood, hay, and stubble certain of the Corinthians could quite easily have recognized themselves. For the community was built of " living stones " (1 Pet. 2: 4-6).

What exactly is meant by " fire "? In the first place simply the judgment. In it all will be revealed at its true worth. A part of this judgment is, of course—in the sense of the Old Testament preaching by the prophets—the preliminaries to the final scene : affliction and persecution. The man who has only run after one or another preacher will have no mind to endure persecution, will have no strength to stand up to pressure.

16Do you not know that you are God's temple and that God's Spirit dwells in you? 17If anyone destroys God's temple, God will destroy him. For God's temple is holy, and that temple you are.

The image of the house becomes that of the temple. As soon as one considers what kind of house the community can be compared with, one thinks of " God's house," more accurately the " temple." But if it is a temple, this can only be the one which uniquely exists in the world for all faithful Israelites—the temple

in Jerusalem. The entire New Testament is borne up by the conviction that the Church has entered into its place, replacing the
house of stone with one of living men, built into a living unity
by the Holy Spirit. He is as much the " spirit of the whole " as
the spirit of each individual. In any case, through him God's
" dwelling " takes on an immediacy and intensity that far out-
strips all previous " dwelling " of God among men. But if this
is true, then the Corinthians must keep in mind the strict law of
holiness that belonged to the temple. Today we are hardly
aware any longer of the seriousness with which all antiquity,
including the pagans, regarded the holiness of temples and re-
acted to any violation of it. It is not for nothing that Paul here
threatens real destruction, while still of course leaving it open
whether, together with the destruction of the flesh, eternal salvation may not be possible (cf. 5 : 5).

The Danger that Wisdom Will Turn into Folly (3:18 23)

¹⁸*Let no one deceive himself. If anyone among you thinks that
he is wise in this age, let him become a fool that he may become
wise.* ¹⁹*For the wisdom of this world is folly with God. For it is
written, " He catches the wise in their craftiness,"* ²⁰*and again,
" The Lord knows that the thoughts of the wise are futile."* ²¹*So
let no one boast of men. For all things are yours,* ²²*whether Paul
or Apollos or Cephas or the world or life or death or the present
or the future, all are yours;* ²³*and you are Christ's; and Christ is
God's.*

This short section deals with two things: a wrong attitude
towards a value good in itself, wisdom; and a wrong attitude
towards persons of (at any rate partial) worth. In this case both

are closely linked and lead to the same significant conclusion, a conclusion all the more significant the less those affected see into it: wisdom turned into folly, freedom into unfreedom. Since the people who impressed the Corinthians were those with wisdom, they staked everything on wisdom (knowledge and culture). But just as in the purely human field it often makes a painful or ludicrous impression when people try to show off the fragments of learning they have picked up, but betray the true state of their knowledge by mispronunciation of names or a false application of concepts, so it happens still more unfailingly before God. Here some think that they know or are something wonderful, but in reality, precisely because of this foolish belief, have become pitiable and ridiculous.

Warnings (4:1–13)

The course of Paul's thoughts is never arranged according to the sense of our logic, in which a single theme is dealt with, point by point. Rather it resembles a weave in which a particular thread appears, remains in sight for a while, then gives way to other threads, but runs on " underground," to be taken up once again and so continued. This is quite especially so in this case where the objective problem (falsely evaluated or applied wisdom) is so mixed with personal elements (the partly good and partly dubious teacher). In the following passage personal viewpoints stand out more sharply in the foreground. They take the form, primarily, of warnings: a warning against rash judgment on pastors of souls (4:1–5); a warning against overestimation of self (4:6–8); and by contrast the Apostle's representation of himself (4:9–13).

Warning against Rash Judgment upon Pastors of Souls (4:1–5)

¹*This is how one should regard us, as servants of Christ and stewards of the mysteries of God.* ²*Moreover it is required of stewards that they be found trustworthy.* ³*But with me it is a very small thing that I should be judged by you or by any human court. I do not even judge myself.* ⁴*I am not aware of anything against myself, but I am not thereby acquitted. It is the Lord who judges me.* ⁵*Therefore do not pronounce judgment before the time, before the Lord comes, who will bring to light the things now hidden in darkness and will disclose the purposes of the heart. Then every man will receive his commendation from God.*

Even in very concrete conflicts and personal explanations the Apostle never forgets that all should draw benefit from his words, including those who are not directly involved in the matter at issue. Conversely, though his vision may have reached out almost into the infinite, this must not tempt him to pass over the concrete situation, which has to be set right in the light of the faith. That is why he now turns his attention back to this situation, not of course in order to repeat himself but to clarify it from a fresh angle. " All are yours "—that is as much as to say that all these are your servants. That it is not too much to say this can be seen from other passages (e.g. 2 Cor. 4:5). But this truth must not be seen in isolation. That is provided for at the end of the same sentence: " and you are Christ's." So you cannot make use of these servants of yours just as you wish. This leads of its own inner logic to the complementary thought that he and his fellow workers are " servants of Christ." Paul extends and deepens this title with another: " stewards of the mysteries of God." In these two parallel constructions " Christ " and " God " correspond to each other, as also do " servants " and " stewards." Perhaps it does not very much matter that the word used here for " servant " (*hyperetes*) was inferior in social standing to " server " (*diakon*), whereas " steward " was superior. When both are related to Christ and to God, they are removed from human judgment.

When Paul says, " I do not even judge myself," this of course does not mean that he practiced no examination of conscience, no self-criticism. But he is certainly conscious of the limits of this self-examination, not because of a defective power of self-understanding, but from more substantial grounds.

Warning against an Overestimation of Self (4:6–8)

⁶*I have applied all this to myself and Apollos for your benefit, brethren, that you may learn by us not to go beyond what is written, that none of you may be puffed up in favor of one against another.* ⁷*For who sees anything different in you? What have you that you did not receive? If then you received it, why do you boast as if it were not a gift?* ⁸*Already you are filled! Already you have become rich! Without us you have become kings! And would that you did reign, so that we might share the rule with you!*

At the beginning of this whole section on Corinthian parties or cliques, the names of four were given (1:12), and at the end three were repeated (3:22). But in the intervening part the longest passage was taken up by the confrontation with Apollos' people. The whole second chapter, dealing with " wisdom," concerned these people with whom " wisdom " played such a large and insidious role. In this matter, however, so far as we can see, Apollos himself is basically as little to blame as is true wisdom itself. In his teaching and manner of preaching there was only a greater danger than with others that a questionable enthusiasm would arise. Paul does not, however, actually choose to blame the damage on him. If he mentions his name several times—together with his own—this is rather to serve as a " model " for the Corinthians, by which it can be made obvious to all what each has to recognize and accept on his own behalf. Paul uses this method in a number of ways, mostly in the manner in which he gives an example in himself of what others ought to learn. In this letter we find the most striking example in the hymn to love (13 : 1ff.).

Out of the two clauses in verse 6 beginning with " that," let us, to start with, leave out of consideration the first, and so go on: " that none of you may be puffed up in favor of one [of us] against another." This means, then, that they should not play off Apollos against Paul, or Paul against Apollos. This is a clear and understandable idea.

" What have you that you did not receive? If then you received it, why do you boast as if it were not a gift?" How often St. Augustine quotes this verse! The Council of Orange, too, in 529, cited it as evidence that none of us is capable of any meritorious work without divine grace. Paul changes the plural " you " in this verse to the singular and thus gives it the most general character—each man can and must let it be said to him. Hence it does not apply only to the graces of service and office that Paul has received in this and Apollos in that manner, but it applies to every grace. Does it not apply to all things whatever, even what we have or are " by nature "? Even if we have gained something by industrious learning and practice, we can only gain it with the powers or talents that have been given us to start with. For the rest we are not forbidden to rejoice in them, or even to " boast "—only we must not forget that we do not have ourselves to thank for them. Insofar as we are to gain an advantage from the talents or graces bestowed on us, we should also acknowledge them. Paul himself did this and gave us a good example of it (3 : 10).

Now the tone changes; Paul becomes ironical. If the Corinthians bear themselves with such self-assurance, as if they had already attained the goal, as if they no longer had to hunger for God's justice and his kingdom, in which the saints are certainly to share in his rule, the Apostle knows that he is still outside, on the way, a pilgrim, and he wishes that he could be taken along with them.

In Contrast, the Apostle's Representation of Himself (4:9–13)

[9]*For I think that God has exhibited us apostles as last of all, like men sentenced to death; because we have become a spectacle to the world, to angels and to men.* [10]*We are fools for Christ's sake, but you are wise in Christ. We are weak, but you are strong. You are held in honor, but we in disrepute.* [11]*To the present hour we hunger and thirst, we are ill-clad and buffeted and homeless,* [12]*and we labor, working with our own hands. When reviled, we bless; when persecuted, we endure;* [13]*when slandered, we try to conciliate; we have become, and are now, as the refuse of the world, the offscouring of all things.*

The self-knowledge of the Apostle, and basically even of the apostles altogether, stands in biting contrast to the self-assurance of the Corinthian community. He is quite satisfied that for him by God's will the position seems, or even is, the other way around, that he rates as last on the usual scale of values, and even far beyond the ordinary bounds like one condemned to death. Jesus was such a one, and such a one Paul had already become in several ways, formally and otherwise. But precisely for Jesus' sake he accepts this life. At that period sentences and their execution were always spectacles for the crowd. Was it not so with Jesus' death? Was it a spectacle also for the angels? They belong to the public willed by God for this drama. Just as Christ's dying means something for these spirits, so too does the dying of his members. Something is enacted here that arouses their deepest amazement, inasmuch as men who by nature are inferior to them receive a far greater glory through the mystery of "dying with Christ."

The More Personal and Forgiving Tone of This Exchange (4:14–21)

The Apostle's Fatherly Love for the Community (4:14–16)

[14]*I do not write this to make you ashamed, but to admonish you as my beloved children.* [15]*For though you have countless guides in Christ, you do not have many fathers. For I became your father in Christ Jesus through the gospel.* [16]*I urge you, then, be imitators of me.*

As in the second letter to the Corinthians, the self-depiction which is not without reproach for those who have required it of him is followed by a striking transition to a loving closeness that must convince us that here a wounded heart has spoken, but one which nevertheless seeks by all means in its power to reach out to the hearts of his beloved children. It put them to shame—he felt it himself—but he would wish it only until they had again come to their senses. After he has let this tone of fatherly love be heard, he gives it yet more emphasis, which indeed immediately calls forth again a comparison with those with whom he can only stress repeatedly the impossibility of comparisons. For what reason could a dozen teachers be against one single father? And Paul says " countless " guides or teachers. One has here to know about the practice of antiquity of providing children with slaves to supervise their studies.

The whole passionate speech echoes in an injunction in which a father's hope is joined with the Apostle's command: " Be imitators of me." In what are they to imitate him? Not in this or that trait of character. They should rather prove themselves his children at heart. Children can sometimes forget themselves, they can come under certain alien influences, but the nature implanted in them will come out. When it comes to the test, children will not deny their parents, especially their fathers. That is the human starting point for this brief warning. The idea of imitation is by no means merely incidental in Paul's mind. What he means by it is more precisely formulated in another passage: " Be imitators of me as I am of Christ."

The Mission of the Apostolic Visitor (4:17)

[17]*Therefore I sent to you Timothy, my beloved and faithful child in the Lord, to remind you of my ways in Christ, as I teach them everywhere in every church.*

This announcement of a *legatus a latere* comes as something of a surprise. Paul does not think it enough to rely on his pastoral letter, penetrating and personal though it is. He " sends " a man who is in his confidence, and has full powers from him. In conformity with what has gone before, Paul stresses less the fullness of power, but much more a true child-like relationship to him, which of course carries with it loyalty to the Lord's cause. The expression with which he defines Timothy's mission is not so general in meaning as it might seem to us. In the Semitic sense " my ways " means not his personal career but his teaching. It means, in effect, the same as the injunction, " Be imitators of me." Over and above this he gives importance to the fact that this is not merely his personal teaching, but the universal catholic teaching. He, the Apostle, teaches in this way " everywhere in every church." Again he brings it home to the Corinthians that they are not alone in the world but have to fit into an ecclesiastical order and submit to ecclesiastical discipline.

The Announcement of His Own Visit (4:18–21)

[18]*Some are arrogant, as though I were not coming to you.* [19]*But I will come to you soon, if the Lord wills, and I will find out not the talk of these arrogant people but their power.* [20]*For the kingdom of God does not consist in talk but in power.* [21]*What do you wish? Shall I come to you with a rod, or with love in a spirit of gentleness?*

The remaining verses of the whole of this first part of the letter leave no doubt that Paul, after he has run through the whole range of personal approaches, is also willing to speak and act officially. For certain people the announcement of his visit becomes something of a threat. Then he will see what these people, who consider themselves so important, are really made of. He gives his opinion of them twice over: they are arrogant; they are playing at talking big. But they will make no impression on him! He will not be taken in by big or fine words. What are words? They can have little or great weight. Even the same words can be weighty or light. They take their specific weight from the truth and living power that supports them. They are like paper money: their value depends on the backing in gold, the presence or absence of which not everyone perceives. Still, with most words it soon comes out what they have to back them up. A man's achievements, his actions, reveal what his words are worth.

ON VARIOUS MORAL ABUSES (5:1—6:20)

After dealing with the subject in which Paul sees the basic fault of the Corinthian community, and since so many have been implicated in it or at least inclined to it, he could have gone on to answer the questions directed to him by the community. First, however, he wanted to clear up certain other points which they apparently had not thought were of concern to the Apostle. But now he makes them aware of their external and internal responsibility as a community of Jesus Christ. There are three instances he brings up: a gross case of immorality, that actually amounts to incest (chap. 5); litigation before pagan courts (6:1-11); and a lax notion of impurity (6:12-20). In none of these cases does Paul confine himself to the immediately necessary measures and comments. They become an occasion for him to illuminate the whole field of morals from a Christian point of view, so that these sections, even if their context has for us been partly superseded, are still full of valuable information for the life of faith and morals.

The Case of Incest and Its Purification by the Community (5:1-13)

The Sinner Must Be Excommunicated (5:1-5)

¹*It is actually reported that there is immorality among you, and of a kind that is not found even among pagans; for a man is*

53

*living with his father's wife. ²And you are arrogant! Ought you
not rather to mourn? Let him who has done this be removed
from among you. ³For though absent in body I am present in
spirit, and as if present, I have already pronounced judgment
⁴in the name of the Lord Jesus on the man who has done such
a thing. When you are assembled, and my spirit is present, with
the power of our Lord Jesus, ⁵you are to deliver this man to
Satan for the destruction of the flesh, that his spirit may be
saved in the day of the Lord Jesus.*

The Apostle now attacks this matter with apparent abruptness.
He does not say that he learned of it through Chloe's people, but
contents himself with the observation that it was being reported.
It is not as if it were not discussed in the community. The evil is
that the situation has remained at the stage of being merely
talked about, when the community should have risen up in
indignation, taken a hand in it and acted. A case of such gross
immorality offended against proper law and good morals even
among the pagans, even though it clearly did not concern the
man's own mother but a second wife of the father who, besides,
was either dead or at least divorced from her.

How could the Church of God not grasp that its election, its
holy calling, was besmirched by this! All those sanctified in Jesus
Christ should have been most deeply distressed and should have
excluded such a sinner from the community, for the honor of
Christ, which now rested with them, since he had called them
into his fellowship (1:9). Now the Apostle takes the initiative.
Now he really takes up the rod that shortly before he had
seemed to threaten only jestingly. He demands that the whole
community in an express act exclude this sinner who had
violated their holiness. That is excommunication in the original

sense. When the sinner is thrust out of the community, he loses the sacraments, indeed even salvation. The sacraments are of their nature sacraments of the Church. To belong to her is a continual sacrament, and one should regard each individual sacrament as a concrete actualization of this membership of the Church.

The Community Must Preserve Its Easter Purity and Newness (5:6–8)

⁶*Your boasting is not good. Do you not know that a little leaven leavens the whole lump?* ⁷*Cleanse out the old leaven that you may be a new lump, as you really are unleavened. For Christ, our paschal lamb, has been sacrificed.* ⁸*Let us, therefore, celebrate the festival, not with the old leaven, the leaven of malice and evil, but with the unleavened bread of sincerity and truth.*

This was addressed to a community that was stiff with self-satisfaction and self-assurance. The Apostle cuts away the excuse that the case of this sinner was, after all, an exception, and that it rested only with this one man. Such a thing has its effects on all. Not that all are led to the same sin, but the moral force of all is weakened by it, so that each becomes more vulnerable at his weakest point. Paul shows how this is so in the generally known and proverbial image of the infective power and danger of leaven. Then there comes into his mind another field in which leaven plays a still more significant role. After the Jewish Pasch and before the eight days of the festival, the old leaven and everything leavened with it had to be cleared out of the house. For the Apostle this becomes an expressive image for the new-ness and oneness appropriate to the Christian. The central statement, which he assumes to be known, " Christ, our paschal lamb, has been sacrificed," is of the utmost importance and the only New Testament evidence that already in apostolic times Christ was understood as the paschal lamb. This means that in practice the whole Old Testament paschal typology was understood in a Christian sense—the great feast of the old covenant commemorating the people's deliverance was carried over into the feast of the new covenant. This leaves open the question of whether this rendering by the author of this letter was occasioned by the forthcoming Easter festival—in which case this text would also be the oldest evidence of a Christian Easter festival—or whether, as is more probable, the whole of Christian life is understood in a paschal sense as life in deliverance, and thus as a festival. The latter is meant in either case—the whole time of salvation since Christ's death is basically a single paschal celebration. That is why Jewish ceremonial can be transposed into the spiritual, personal, and existential fields.

This newness and purity cannot be produced by men. It is a gift of grace. That being so, it is of course also required of them. The duty of living anew grows out of the fact of having become new. First, it is true, comes the command " Cleanse out!" But the Apostle is quick to add the basis upon which alone this command is possible, the basis which God himself has created. Grace always precedes our will: " You really are unleavened."

The Community Has the Strict Obligation to Apply Ecclesiastical Sanctions against Public Sinners (5:9–13)

[9]*I wrote to you in my letter not to associate with immoral men;* [10]*not at all meaning the immoral of this world, or the greedy and*

robbers, or idolaters, since then you would need to go out of the world. [11]But rather I wrote to you not to associate with anyone who bears the name of brother if he is guilty of immorality or greed, or is an idolater, reviler, drunkard, or robber—not even to eat with such a one. [12]For what have I to do with judging outsiders? Is it not those inside the church whom you are to judge? [13]God judges those outside. " Drive out the wicked person from among you."

What the Apostle requires of the community with respect to those who relapse into such sins is again nothing less than a sort of excommunication, though certainly a milder one than that solemnly introduced earlier. Such people might no longer take part in communal meals, whether or not joined with the eucharist. They should also be avoided at less formal gatherings and excluded from more friendly invitations. They should be made aware that they have made themselves unworthy of the name of Christians. The eucharist is still understood as a family meal, while every meal among friends who are Christians has in it something of the Lord's supper.

No one in the community may dispense himself in this matter, as if the public sins of others were no concern of his. Here there can be no comfortable flight into detachment, any more than it can be said within a family : What my brother does is no concern of mine, am I then my brother's keeper? To be sure, Church discipline, to be practicable, presupposed the existence of communities taking charge, which can still see themselves as large families. In this sense the Apostle can say that the Church does not have to judge " outsiders." This does not contradict the statement that follows shortly, that the saints will judge the world on that day when everything will be revealed. Now the grace is given and with it the duty of judging themselves before that inescapable judgment, and of seeing that all may be found blameless.

So far as the separation of " inside " and " outside " is concerned, this has become more difficult for us. Nevertheless, it has not fallen away altogether. We can, it is true, no longer determine the boundaries of the Church with the same certainty, because membership has many gradations, so that towards the margin one can almost say that there are no longer any boundaries any more. But in practice, for the concrete responsibility that the Apostle emphasizes here, these boundaries certainly still exist. They are fixed according to the possibility of an effective sharing in responsibility. This too can again be graded—direct influence may be limited to a few, but prayer and expiatory sharing of responsibility can include everybody.

Legal Proceedings by Christians before Pagan Courts (6:1–11)

Christians Should Not Bring Each Other Before Pagan Courts (6:1–6)

[1]*When one of you has a grievance against a brother, does he dare go to law before the unrighteous instead of the saints?* [2]*Do you not know that the saints will judge the world? And if the world is to be judged by you, are you incompetent to try trivial cases?* [3]*Do you not know that we are to judge angels? How much more, matters pertaining to this life!* [4]*If then you have such cases, why do you lay them before those who are least esteemed by the church?* [5]*I say this to your shame. Can it be that there is no man*

*among you wise enough to decide between members of the
brotherhood, ⁶but brother goes to law against brother, and that
before unbelievers?*

Paul has just been dealing with spiritual judgment and reminding the community of its duty in relation to it. This is an opportunity for him to discuss a matter that has indeed to do with
judgment, but on a quite different plane. While the community
had culpably failed in one respect, they had also culpably failed
in another. The evil is twofold: they have grievances over every-
day matters, and on account of these they bring each other
before pagan courts. It is this last that strikes the Apostle as so
impossible. Small though the Christian community was in this
great city, people everywhere had still heard of it and knew that
these men had been converted to a strict religion. And that they
led a communal life as brothers and sisters. What an annihilating effect it must have on the public—and the courts were of
their nature public—if " brothers " quarreled with each other in
the courts and brought their respective witnesses with them. We
can sympathize with the Apostle in his raising of this matter.
But there was something else too in which we can no longer
altogether feel with him. He lived in awareness of the imminent
judgment of the world. In his mission he knew himself as
already the messenger of the coming Judge of the world. For
him there was added to this the idea, which Jesus also confirmed
to the Apostles, that the elect would share in the judging. When
he asks: " Do you not know that the saints will judge the
world? ", we can see that this eschatological orientation towards
the early return of the Lord occupied an important place in his
preaching. This letter in particular confirms this in almost all the
themes discussed. Paul's direction concerning such worldly

quarrels corresponds to the teaching of Jesus in the sermon on
the mount (Mt. 5:25).

Christians Should Not Go to Law at All (6:7–8)

*7To have lawsuits at all with one another is defeat for you. Why
not rather suffer wrong? Why not rather be defrauded? 8But you
yourselves wrong and defraud, and that even your own brethren.*

With his " at all " Paul begins to look beyond the immediate
issue to be settled and to consider the matter from a more comprehensive and penetrating viewpoint. For Christians ought not
all these disputed things—a little bit of property, of justice, of
honor—really be far too trivial measured against God's riches
and God's honor, in which they shared? And should they not be
afraid, in thus fighting for their rights, of doing injustice to
others? The sentence " Why not rather suffer wrong? " may
remind one of Socrates, though much more, as a whole, of the
spirit and letter of the sermon on the mount (cf. Mt. 5:20, 40).
What is at stake in this " at all " is more than justice in earthly
things. It is that God's superabundant justice may come through,
so that we may prove ourselves children of the heavenly father,
at any rate those who under him see themselves as brothers.

Christians Must Know that They Have Left the Vices of the World Behind Them (6:9–11)

*9Do you not know that the unrighteous will not inherit the king-
dom of God? Do not be deceived; neither the immoral, nor*

idolaters, nor adulterers, nor homosexuals, [10]*nor thieves, nor the greedy, nor drunkards, nor revilers, nor robbers will inherit the kingdom of God.* [11]*And such were some of you. But you were washed, you were sanctified, you were justified in the name of the Lord Jesus Christ and in the Spirit of our God.*

There is a great danger that through worldly things people will let themselves be drawn back again into the " unrighteousness " of the world. Paul previously used the phrase " the unrighteous " to describe the pagan judges (6:1). Here it becomes clearer that he also wants to underline the anomaly of " justified " Christians seeking justice from such as these. The man who holds to the unrighteousness of the world loses the " kingdom of God." It is characteristic that this central concept of the message of Jesus, which only occasionally occurs in Paul, is met with here where he is repeating the moral precepts of Jesus as he had delivered them in his missionary preaching.

What Paul lists here has the appearance of a confessional mirror held up to " grave sins " which concerned the Corinthians. Those who were converted as a result of his missionary preaching laid out their lives before him, and he had to make clear to them what were the vices to be absolutely shunned. From these general confessions he came to know the whole depravity of the life of the great city of Corinth. The ten vices that he lists here are again divided between the sixth and seventh commandments. They knew it. He needed only to remind them of it quite carefully : " Such were some of you." But he does not leave it at that. That is the past that has been wiped out. In a triple phrase he calls upon the experience and the effect of their baptism. One is almost reminded of the trinitarian baptismal formula when he closes this baptismal reminder with the names of the Son and the Holy Spirit, whom he describes as " the Spirit of our God."

Against Lax Notions of Impurity (6:12–20)

The Body Is More than the Stomach (6:12–14)

¹²*"All things are lawful for me," but not all things are helpful. " All things are lawful for me," but I will not be enslaved by anything.* ¹³*" Food is meant for the stomach and the stomach for the food "—and God will destroy both one and the other. The body is not meant for immorality, but for the Lord and the Lord for the body.* ¹⁴*And God raised the Lord and will also raise us up by his power.*

" All things are lawful for me." Without transition, and yet in continuation of the serious warning not to deceive oneself, Paul takes up a phrase that plays an insidious role in Corinth. He himself may have formulated his doctrine of freedom in Christ in this way. But just as chapter 3 says not only " All things are yours " (verse 21) but also " and you are Christ's " (verse 23), so he said also to the Galatians: " For you were called to freedom, brethren; only do not use your freedom as an opportunity for the flesh " (Gal. 5 : 13).

" The body is not meant for immorality but for the Lord." This total belonging to the Lord deeply conditions the Apostle's self-understanding, and he considers it should be so for every Christian. " None of us lives to himself, and none of us dies to himself. If we live, we live to the Lord, and if we die, we die to the Lord " (Rom. 14 : 7).

Paul once more takes a surprising step when he dares to reverse the phrase here too: ". . . and the Lord for the body." We need only to take seriously the bodily eucharistic gift of himself to us by the Lord to see this mutual relationship bodily confirmed. And if it had to be said earlier that " God will destroy both one and the other," now it is said that as he raised up the Lord, so he will raise us too in our bodies, and thus once and for all confirm that belonging together which the sacraments now attest. That is why any misuse of our bodily existence is a sin against the original calling of the believer, a misuse of the power of sex and an attack on the rights of the Lord, as if it were his own body. Thus in questions of purity the bodily, all-embracing, and total belonging to Christ is intensified.

Immorality in the Baptized Is a Profaning of Christ (6:15–17)

[15]*Do you not know that your bodies are members of Christ? Shall I therefore take the members of Christ and make them members of a prostitute? Never!* [16]*Do you not know that he who joins himself to a prostitute becomes one body with her? For, as it is written, " The two shall become one."* [17]*But he who is united to the Lord becomes one spirit with him.*

Now the Apostle speaks more precisely of the kind of immorality that was practiced by certain Corinthians in such a fatal manner. The problem of prostitution. One has to realize here that among the ancient Greeks monogamy was indeed in force as the natural legal system, but that the wife was primarily the housekeeper and mother of legitimate children. She was by no means so greatly esteemed as a person that living with her could provide fulfillment for the man. What was missing in the marriage or lacking in excitement men sought to satisfy with prostitutes or courtesans, if not in homosexual relations. Here Paul speaks only of the relationship with prostitutes.

The aforementioned belonging to Christ he first of all applies more concretely: our bodies are " members of Christ." So those who go to a prostitute make the members of Christ members of a prostitute. Christ and the prostitute suddenly and frighteningly confront each other. But there is no way out into neutrality, there is no no-man's land. As a matter of fact there is one case Paul leaves completely out of account here: the legitimate fulfillment of marriage in which the union of the couple is not synonymous with a withdrawal from Christ but their mutual giving can, may, and should at the same time be a giving to Christ.

The Body of the Baptized Man Is a Temple of the Holy Spirit
(6 : 18–20)

[18]*Shun immorality. Every other sin which a man commits is outside the body; but the immoral man sins against his own body.* [19]*Do you not know that your body is a temple of the Holy Spirit within you, which you have from God? You are not your own;* [20]*you were bought with a price. So glorify God in your body.*

Paul sums up and repeats the result of his previous argument in the short sentence " Shun immorality!" And with this he goes on to establish another point. But is it right that every other sin is " outside the body "? Drunkards or suicides also act against the body. Still, everyone in fact understands what Paul means. Impurity takes place not only in the body but with the body. The deeper reason why impurity is felt to be more a matter of the body, more physical than any other sin, does not of course lie in the body as such but in the fact that precisely in impurity, in sexual activity, body and spirit, body and person, body and self, can be less separate than in any other action.

ANSWERS TO VARIOUS QUESTIONS FROM THE COMMUNITY (7:1—14:40)

On Marriage and Virginity (7:1–40)

Paul goes into a number of particular cases in order partly to point to binding commandments of the Lord, and partly to give advice according to the mind and spirit of Jesus, recommendations and directions in which he comes to grips with the dangers facing this young missionary community but in which, too, is brought to light in all kinds of ways what the world has to thank Christianity for. One is repeatedly amazed at how Paul is able to combine two things—to proclaim the destiny of man which exceeds all that is human, and at the same time to do justice to the human reality.

The Most Important and Fundamental Clarification, above All Concerning Marriage (7:1–7)

Right and Necessity of Marriage as the Normal Condition even of Christians (7:1–2)

[1]Now concerning the matters about which you wrote. It is well for a man not to touch a woman. [2]But because of the temptation to immorality, each man should have his own wife and each woman her own husband.

Paul takes for granted the vocation to virginity, for the reasons already given and later made clearer (7 : 7). Strictly speaking, what we have called by anticipation virginity is here only negatively defined as sexual continence. The statement is framed in a general way to concern " men " and this includes, in principle, the female sex also, but in practice only the man's part is then described—the man who does not touch a woman. At that time, there was as yet no positive name for the single state, neither " virginity " nor " celibacy." Jesus, too, could only formulate his summons in negative terms (Mt. 19 : 11f.).

" Well " (*kalon*) means here what stands on a high ethical level, is praiseworthy in itself, is completely to be approved. Later in the chapter Paul will give more precise reasons for this high estimation of celibacy or virginity. First he hastens to bring the Corinthians down to earth by reminding them of the fact that not all can manage this continence. If they were to live this ideal badly, then a normal marriage would be preferable. In itself, continence may be better, but for many people marriage is better. The man who fails here falls lower. The one who lives rightly here wins salvation thereby.

" Each man " and " each woman " does not mean all without exception, but only those who cannot be exceptional. But it is true without exception that each husband should have his own wife, and each wife her own husband. This sets out clearly two principal characteristics of marriage, oneness and indissolubility.

MAN AND WIFE HAVE THE SAME RIGHTS AND THE SAME DUTIES IN MARRIAGE (7:3–4)

³*The husband should give to his wife her conjugal rights, and likewise the wife to her husband.* ⁴*For the wife does not rule*

over her own body, but the husband does; likewise the husband does not rule over his own body, but the wife does.

The Apostle is not afraid of saying very concretely what it means to have a wife and to have a husband, and to call each other man and wife. The phrase in which he sums up his instruction is "conjugal rights." From here he moves into the law and morality of marriage, and into common speech. Among Christians as among all men, what makes up the essence of marriage is the mutual giving of rights over the body. The right of the one corresponds to the duty of the other and vice versa. The still greater importance of this verse, however, is that nowhere else in all antiquity is the equality of man and wife in these marital matters so expressly proclaimed. It could not be when simultaneous or successive polygamy prevailed formally or in practice. It was certainly far from being so when monogamy was recognized and allowed in legal terms only.

TEMPORARY CONTINENCE IS TO BE RECOMMENDED FOR SPIRITUAL REASONS (7:5)

[5]Do not refuse one another except perhaps by agreement for a season, that you may devote yourselves to prayer; but then come together again, lest Satan tempt you through lack of self-control.

This verse is perhaps even more surprising than the two that precede it. It shows again clearly how far the married in Corinth went in their zeal. Some of their own accord renounced marital union and took it for granted that their partner was also capable of this. Paul approves such marital continence under three conditions. It must be for the sake of a spiritual good. It must come from mutual agreement. And it must be limited. This last point can be explained by concern at the temptation which might otherwise become too great, of the one party who did not match the other in moral and spiritual strength. Nothing is said here of the length of this agreed time. The married people of the time had to clarify this between themselves. The important thing is that married people recognize of their own accord how beneficial and even necessary temporary marital abstinence is for them. The conjugal right must not become an enslavement, nor a devalued routine. The marital union should be strong also on the spiritual side, in order, with the spirit, to make the body and the spiritual life free for God.

MARRIAGE AND VIRGINITY: TWO GIFTS OF GRACE (7:6-7)

[6]I say this by way of concession, not of command. [7]I wish that all were as I myself am. But each has his own special gift from God, one of one kind and one of another.

It is somewhat difficult to decide whether this distinction between concession and command, which the Apostle very conscientiously and very wisely undertakes, refers only to verse 5 or to verse 2. This situation is often met with in Paul's writings. Such a verse is attached immediately to that preceding it and its content is determined by it, but at the same time it leads on to the next and is also partly determined by that. Verse 7 corresponds in its second half very closely to the second halves of verses 1 and 2 (cf. the use of " each "). The later sentence, to be sure, goes far beyond what has been said in the earlier verses. If before, marriage could appear as only a necessary evil, here it is raised to the dignity of a " charisma." One should not take the expression " charisma " here in absolutely the same sense as later in chapter 12, but it remains a positive statement. In any case, grace is acknowledged thereby as playing some part in marriage. Marriage and virginity are not states that a man can choose for, or force upon, himself. He is chosen and called for either by the disposition of God. And it is just this that ultimately forms the basis of the good in either condition. Paul does not by any means thereby level out the difference in the standing of the two that he has set up right at the beginning, and to which he again testifies in a wholly personal way, but he subjects it too to the disposition of God.

Consequences for Particular Marriage Cases (7:8–16)

FREEDOM TO MARRY, COMMITMENT IN MARRIAGE (7:8–11)

[8]*To the unmarried and the widows I say that it is well for them to remain single as I do.* [9]*But if they cannot exercise self-control, they should marry. For it is better to marry than to be aflame with passion.*

[10]*To the married I give charge, not I but the Lord, that the wife should not separate from her husband* [11]*(but if she does, let her remain single or else be reconciled to her husband)—and that the husband should not divorce his wife.*

In his introductory sentence Paul has intentionally chosen the most general expression: " It is well for a man." Now he sets to work to apply to particular groups what he has said in general. In the first instance he has in mind members of the Christian community, starting again with the unmarried or widowed, then the married. He repeats his first basic statement of what is definitely good, i.e., to remain unmarried, and after that what *in some circumstances* is nevertheless better, i.e., to marry if continence is too difficult for someone. Fine though it is to be free for the Lord, this decision and condition would be senseless if in practice it became a continual unfreedom, a constant unrest and a lasting enslavement to sexual desire. Paul only speaks of this as he spoke earlier of the danger of immorality. The choice must be made according to what is better with regard to salvation, not according to the preferences of human, worldly, and social advantage or opportunity.

That Paul presupposes the basic readiness for such an attitude, and even its actual existence in the Corinthian community, seems apparent from what follows. There must have been married people—in particular women—who out of such striving for perfection wanted to give up their marriages. The Apostle impresses upon them the strict command of Jesus, which we know from the Gospel (Mt. 5:32; 19:9), and which Paul knew and faithfully preached and taught either from oral tradition or from a collection of sayings of the Lord. Whereas before the choice was between what was good in itself and what in certain circumstances was better, here no choice is left. Here the plain will of the Lord applies, and without exception.

Paul does indeed know of and recognize a possible separation of spouses. There can be cases where the continuance of life together is not to be expected. Then, Paul explains, separation from bed and board is allowed, but not entry into a new marriage. The bond of marriage remains, even if married life together is suspended. Thus reconciliation is always possible, but remarriage never. Paul lays this down in the first place for women who were or might be tempted to release themselves from their marital bond. This was permitted them according to Greek and Roman law, whereas in Jewish law divorce could come only from the man. That is why we read here the prohibition: " the husband should not divorce his wife."

TWO DIFFERENT POSSIBILITIES FOR MARRIAGES IN WHICH ONE PARTY REMAINS AN UNBELIEVER (*Privilegium Paulinum*) (7:12-16)

[12]*To the rest I say, not the Lord, that if any brother has a wife who is an unbeliever, and she consents to live with him, he should not divorce her.* [13]*If any woman has a husband who is an unbeliever, and he consents to live with her, she should not divorce him.* [14]*For the unbelieving husband is consecrated through his wife, and the unbelieving wife is consecrated through her husband. Otherwise, your children would be unclean, but as it is they are holy.* [15]*But if the unbelieving partner desires to separate, let it be so; in such a case the brother or sister is not bound. For God has called us to peace.* [16]*Wife, how do you know whether you will save your husband? Husband, how do you know whether you will save your wife?*

The next case that Paul takes under consideration is harder to clear up. It certainly affected quite a few marriages in the Corinthian community. It was not to be expected that both parties to an existing marriage would always become Christians together. We know of enough examples from early Christian documents and legends, and not only from the early Christian period but also from the later time of the conversion of the German tribes. And today too, of course, in all parts of the missionary field. When a spouse becomes a Christian, this affects the marriage more deeply than if he had joined any other union or movement, because Christian faith represents such a definite teaching on marriage. It may be that this lofty and beautiful but also strict notion of marriage, which the partner inclining to or going over to the Christian community brings into the home, suggests to the still pagan partner, perhaps even decides for him, to turn to this teaching himself. However, the opposite can also arise. Jesus said nothing about this very concrete situation. How should he have taken a position on all situations that might arise in the future? For this purpose he has endowed his Church with his spirit and with full powers from him. It belongs to the task and grace of the apostolic office to decide such questions according to the mind of Jesus and with his authority.

What then does Paul decide? He decides on principle for the continuance of such marriages. He lays this down just as strictly as he previously introduced the general prohibition on divorce as a teaching of Jesus. He formulates his teaching twice in similar terms: for the Christian husband who has an unbelieving wife, and for the Christian wife who has an unbelieving husband. This again deserves special attention because divorce was otherwise never seen as belonging to the wife. So in this prohibition of divorce, the equality of man and woman is expressed most emphatically. The following condition or presupposition is added: if the unbelieving party would like to maintain the marriage. A certain possibility remains open which Paul will deal with later.

First, the Apostle gives a reason for this decision that surprises us in several respects. How is the unbelieving partner "consecrated" by the believing partner? Probably some Corinthians had argued in precisely the opposite sense: it was inadmissible, unfitting, or not to be expected that one sanctified in Christ should live with an unbeliever. And had not Paul said earlier that a little leaven would leaven the whole lump, that is, make it bad? Yes, but precisely at that point he had also emphasized that this strict separation must follow towards "anyone who bears the name of brother" but not towards "outsiders" (5:6–13). And here the case is different again. Here the believer is bound to the unbeliever by a tie made sacred by the Creator. Paul does not refer back expressly to the order of creation in which the natural sanctity of marriage is grounded, but one can best understand his thought from this point of view. And since he has just referred to Jesus' prohibition of divorce, one can and indeed must assume that he had in mind the whole of the Lord's saying in which Jesus wishes explicitly to restore what was "in the beginning," according to the story of creation. Then there fall to the ground certain attempts at forced explanations which seek to find a magical understanding of a "holiness" that is transmitted by bodily contact. It is not yet, of course, a question of the holiness that is afforded by baptism as an inner participation in God's Holy Spirit. But the pagan party to a marriage is already to some extent taken into the Christian community by the fully sanctified partner with whom he is willing to remain together. There is no hint of the fear that the believing party would be better loosed from the attachment to the unbelieving, no hint of the fear that the believing party might be brought to relapse! Would we not today be more likely to feel the matter in these terms, and to advise and decide accordingly? How small in faith we have become compared with this trust in grace! And yet the hope is not even expressed here of winning the unbelieving party for the faith. It is not a question of calculation, only the conviction of the greater power of Christian reality which is not a human power, but God's power.

Now, however, the Apostle adds a further strong point to his argument which, if possible, causes us even more surprise. This is the reference to the fact that the children of such a marriage with a pagan are not unclean or unsanctified, but, on the contrary, " holy." Again we have to ask upon what grounds are these children to be regarded by the Apostle as holy. Certainly not by reason of their baptism, for infant baptism can in no sense be taken for granted here. This holiness is rather a call for baptism, a certain anticipatory relation to baptism. Let us first notice that here children are discussed only in relation to marriage questions. It may surprise us that this had not happened earlier. The way in which they are mentioned shows them as belonging as a matter of course to marriage and therefore naturally having a part in its holiness. We must conclude that such children were regarded as already belonging in some way to the community. What is said here cannot be a mere play upon ideas. It is, on the contrary, an argument perceptible to and enlightening for everyone. If you already treat the children as belonging, how can the marital partner not be included too?

Now Paul goes into the other question, where the unbelieving party wants to be divorced. Paul is not able or willing to restrain him. For he has no word from the Lord. To cling tenaciously to such a marriage is in the last analysis impossible, any basis for it is lacking. Even though we find these reasons illuminating, we can nevertheless not draw from them the conclusions that Paul here draws, with full apostolic powers—the Christian spouse is also free. Because it is an exception, in contradiction to the strict principle, this ruling has received the title *"Privilegium Paulinum."* It is still often today applied in missionary countries, and also occasionally among ourselves, where its use may increase in the future, since the number of the unbaptized is growing in the former Christian countries.

" For God has called us to peace." This sentence summarizes a great deal. The peace to which God has called us through faith and baptism is in the first instance peace with himself, the same peace that the angels proclaimed at the birth of the Saviour. But this peace will and should be experienced also horizontally. Men who have been redeemed should grant it to each other, should bring it to pass among themselves in proportion to their closeness to the original source of all peace in God. Who should have more opportunity for this than married people who are joined in the closest living union together? But of course for this very reason they can also deprive each other most horribly of all peace if they come into conflict over what alone can most deeply unite them.

Vocation and Profession: On the Relation of Christianity to the Secular Order (7:17–24)

THE EXAMPLE OF CIRCUMCISION: A CONTRIBUTION ON THE PROBLEM OF THE JEWS (7:17–19)

¹⁷Only, let every one lead the life which the Lord has assigned to him, and in which God has called him. This is my rule in all the churches.

Basically what is pointed out here is a reference to God's ordinance: if your condition was such that the call of God's grace could reach you in it, if it was right for God's purpose, then it should be right for you thereafter. The dress that a girl wore the first time her future husband saw her, she will never think lightly of. The bridegroom too will treasure it for the same reason. On the part of those called, therefore, there is a tender gratitude for the grace of their calling, which means a freedom in relation to all earthly things, as Paul has already described in this letter: " All things are yours . . ." It expresses also an attitude that corresponds to the well-known saying of Jesus: " Render therefore to Caesar the things that are Caesar's, and to God the things that are God's " (Mt. 22:21). An important reason for this can be added on another level. It could not at that point fall to the Church to topple the entire social structure. But that is precisely what would have come about if the Christian teaching of freedom had been changed into a general cry for freedom. Certainly this prescription was not to be binding in every individual case. The rule was to be valid as a general guideline, which presupposed that the trade, occupation, or business in which the person concerned found himself was honorable in itself.

[18]Was anyone at the time of his call already circumcised? Let him not seek to remove the marks of circumcision. Was anyone at the time of his call uncircumcised? Let him not seek circumcision. [19]For neither circumcision counts for anything nor uncircumcision, but keeping the commandments of God.

Paul now illustrates the basic principle set out above from two cases which in Corinth were of great relevance. According to all that we know of this community, people were very much inclined to draw radical conclusions. Had Paul given free play to this tendency, Christianity would have become an upheaval, a movement religiously based certainly, but nevertheless tearing down all boundaries, overturning all relationships, dissolving all order. Paul sets up a barrier against this—the doctrine of " state of life." " State " has to be understood here in a quite general sense that can mean equally the ethnic or social or legal or economic position. The first concrete situation Paul tackles concerns the pagan or Jewish origin of members of the community. From the point of view of soteriology it is and remains a fundamental justification of the Church's existence that it consists of Jews and Gentiles—of Jews, so that continuity of God's promise is shown, and of Gentiles so that the extension of this promise and with it the universality of his will to salvation is revealed. But precisely for this reason the Jew should not be ashamed of his origin. Of course, the Gentile too should not think that he must make a detour through Judaism. In Paul's missionary communities there were at that time tendencies towards and attempts at requiring both the one and the other. He had at times to proceed more sharply, in particular against the latter movement.

THE EXAMPLE OF SLAVERY: A CONTRIBUTION ON THE SOCIAL QUESTION (7:20–24)

[20]*Every one should remain in the state in which he was called.* [21]*Were you a slave when called? Never mind. But if you can gain your freedom, avail yourself of the opportunity.* [22]*For he who was called in the Lord as a slave is a freedman of the Lord. Likewise he who was free when called is a slave of Christ.*[23]*You were bought with a price; do not become slaves of men.* [24]*So, brethren, in whatever state each was called, there let him remain with God.*

The second example with which Paul expresses his basic principle was much more far-reaching for the state and the social order as a whole in antiquity—the slaves. Here we find more explicitly than in 1:26–28, where the composition of the community was also discussed, that slaves belonged to it. Slaves were for the most part more numerous than free men in the households, workshops, and businesses of citizens. If the proclamation of freedom had been misunderstood by them, this would perhaps have compelled the state to suppress Christianity by force. Paul does not only say in general that slaves should remain as they were. He even seems to add (in one rendering) that if one of them has the opportunity to become free, he should see a greater gain for himself in remaining a slave. How great must the happiness of the slaves have been that they were full members of the Christian community, were treated as brothers and sisters by those who were free, for them to accept this prescription! How great must have been their readiness for the highest spiritual values derived from following Jesus in obedience and self-sacrifice! There were surely also cases in which both slaves and their masters became Christians. In this ideal case true brotherhood was easier to realize. In other cases, however, it was certainly harder, whether this difficulty was caused by the whole nature of the state of slavery, the Christian insufficiency of the slaves, or that of the masters.

This teaching by no means led to the permanent preservation of slavery, as one would perhaps have to assume at first. Its removal did indeed take time, and in some places certainly too much time, but it really contributed to it. So too Paul in no way made any general proclamation of the equal rights of women, for which mankind at that time was not yet ready. But what he taught in practice in matters of marital conduct already contained equality of rights and only needed time to penetrate gradually from the innermost circle into the whole relationship of the sexes.

Clarifications Concerning Voluntary Celibacy (7:25–35)

RECOMMENDATION OF CELIBACY (7 : 25–28)

[25]*Now concerning the unmarried, I have no command of the Lord, but I give my opinion as one who by the Lord's mercy is trustworthy.* [26]*I think that in view of the impending distress it is well for a person to remain as he is.* [27]*Are you bound to a wife? Do not seek to be free. Are you free from a wife? Do not seek marriage.* [28]*But if you marry, you do not sin, and if a girl marries she does not sin. Yet those who marry will have worldly troubles, and I would spare you that.*

Paul knows the high values set upon virginity freely chosen and maintained for the kingdom of heaven's sake. It is, of course, not a command by which the question would be decided in advance. Paul presupposes this negative assertion. The Corinthians too must learn to distinguish between what is absolutely to be held and believed, so that there can be no further discussion of it, and truths and directives that are not binding in the same degree, although they are by no means completely given over to choice. Catholic teaching does justice to this fact by the distinction it makes between command and precept. So in this matter Paul puts forward his opinion and bases his advice on the fact that he deserves credence by reason of his mission and work. What he has to say over and above the basic recommendation to celibacy given in the first sentence of this chapter, which is made with an eye to both sexes from the start, is here contained in the argument " in view of the impending distress." It is not easy to decide whether what is meant is the eschatological distress that the Apostle holds to be imminent, or whether this expression, like the coming " troubles," always relates to the given situation of the Church in a world alien to God. Even the future tense—" those who marry will have worldly troubles "—does not conclusively favor the eschatological interpretation. It could also refer to the fact that those who marry will be more exposed to the onslaught of the hostile world as a result of their family ties. It is, however, certain that the situation of persecution always has something eschatological in it and that in the actual, final and truly eschatological time, this advice will apply to the highest degree.

THE SPIRIT OF DETACHMENT OR VIRGINITY REQUIRED OF ALL (7:29–31)

[29]*I mean, brethren, the appointed time has grown very short; from now on, let those who have wives live as though they had none,* [30]*and those who mourn as though they were not mourning, and those who rejoice as though they were not rejoicing, and those who buy as though they had no goods,* [31]*and those who deal with the world as though they had no dealings with it. For the form of this world is passing away.*

Again the Apostle looks beyond the immediate question to what is universally valid. What he says by way of introduction is the main point from which all that follows proceeds. He says it therefore with solemn emphasis, so that one might almost translate it as " this is my explanation." The closing sentence of this short extract has to be seen as a continuation and clarification of this explanation that the time is now but short: " For the form of this world is passing away." By this can only be meant the coming end of the world. But is it still valid if this end of the world has now been delayed for nineteen-hundred years? We must distinguish between what the Apostle personally may well have thought, and even held as certain, in the question of the final judgment, and what, independently of this opinion and beyond it, should remain valid as a teaching for the whole Church. But the same applies also to the teaching of Jesus. And does it not apply everywhere to all the words of scripture? They take for granted specific presuppositions and are addressed to specific situations, and yet preserve a validity for other times and circumstances. It is not always easy to extricate this enduring validity from the circumstances of the original situation. But precisely in this lies the task of exposition for which the Holy Spirit is promised us. It remains valid to say that since the first coming of the Son of man, the world stands under a different sign. It seems to go on existing as before, and yet it is different. It is as if gripped between the first coming and the Lord's return. The phrase that, for the sake of simplicity, is here translated as " short " means something like this: The situations now to be discussed are similarly gripped between these two short sentences that say so much.

What is meant by " Let those who have wives live as though they had none "? It cannot mean the opposite of what the Apostle had proposed to married people at the very beginning, as the norm for their life together. So it does not mean simply a renunciation of marital union, or even a way of life that is totally lacking in concern for one's partner. But they certainly should not be so much at the mercy of their marital relations that they could not exist without them. There must be an area of freedom, as is indicated here, and by no means for the first time. The advice to renounce physical union by agreement for a time in order to devote themselves to prayer already pointed in the same direction.

WHERE THE ADVANTAGE OF THE VIRGIN STATE LIES (7:32–35)

[32]*I want you to be free from anxieties. The unmarried man is anxious about the affairs of the Lord;* [33]*but the married man is anxious about worldly affairs, how to please his wife,* [34]*and his interests are divided. And the unmarried woman or girl is anxious about the affairs of the Lord, how to be holy in body and spirit; but the married woman is anxious about worldly affairs, how to please her husband.* [35]*I say this for your own benefit, not to lay any restraint upon you, but to promote good order and to secure your undivided devotion to the Lord.*

After the self-contained section 7:29–31, the Apostle takes up again the preceding idea of " sparing " them. The relationship of the two passages is made especially recognizable in that he again says here " I want." The new point in this passage, which is similarly a unity, lies in the reference to anxieties, the word " anxious " or " anxieties " being used five times. It occurs in two different ways. First it is used, so to say, negatively, as in the sermon on the mount. It speaks of conduct that is forbidden to the Christian. He is free of the things about which the world is concerned, and thus of the anxieties typical of the world. He has another anxiety—for the things of the Lord. Now, however, the married person moves into a situation of conflicting obliga-tions. Besides being " anxious "—on the one hand for the things of the Lord, on the other for those of the world—a second distinctive word here used is " to please "—on the one hand the Lord, on the other his wife (or her husband).

Opposed to the anxiety over the things of the world, negatively defined, is the anxiety for the things of the Lord. What is the opposite of being divided? We should like to answer: belonging undividedly to the Lord. This, however, is not there. Or is it perhaps there, only in a somewhat different form? It does in fact seem that the statement " how to be holy in body and spirit " represents precisely such a correspondence. It is not as if married people could not and must not also be holy. But the Apostle is here looking for a phrase to mean especially and exclusively belonging to the Lord, being at his disposal, and he sums it up in these words. The last verse, which lies a little outside the otherwise regular series of parallels, contains principally the effort to express this positive idea.

Final Detailed Advice for Two Special Groups (7:36–40)

To Fathers of Grown-Up Daughters (7:36–38)

[36]*If anyone thinks that he is not behaving properly towards his betrothed, if his passions are strong, and it has to be, let him do as he wishes : let them marry—it is no sin.* [37]*But whoever is firmly established in his heart, being under no necessity but having his desire under control, and has determined this in his heart, to keep her as his betrothed, he will do well.* [38]*So that he who marries his betrothed does well; and he who refrains from marriage will do better.*

The basic line in what Paul says here has long since been laid down. Its development in this particular case seems to us strangely harsh or forced or complex, perhaps because we do not know exactly the circumstances or the form of the inquiry. The most important key to understanding lies in the patriarchal family system. The passage refers to the father or guardian, perhaps also the uncle or the oldest brother, to whomever belonged the responsibility for the marriageable daughter, the arrangement of her marriage according to law and custom. If someone in this position finds that custom pressingly requires the marriage of the girl, he should do what he judges he cannot avoid—he does not sin. But if he has the power to decide according to his own ideas, he may do what Paul has explained throughout the whole chapter as better: keep the girl completely for the Lord. The girl's agreement is here taken for granted as it was in the Middle Ages when children were married off by their parents or put into the cloister. For us today this is a crying injustice. What appears as such today was not so in quite different circumstances. Paul did a great deal for the equal rights of women. What he writes here simply takes account of the given circumstances. What was to happen to grown-up daughters was at that time reckoned not according to their own feelings or wishes but according to social custom, which even today still plays its part. Just as Paul did not want radically to overturn the status of the slaves, so it is here with the family system.

To Widows (7:39-40)

[39]*A wife is bound to her husband as long as he lives. If the husband dies, she is free to be married to whom she wishes, only*

in the Lord. ⁴⁰But in my judgment she is happier if she remains as she is. And I think that I have the Spirit of God.

With a widow the case is different. First Paul asserts again the indissolubility of marriage, till death divides. He uses an expression for death (in some versions) that has subsequently remained part of the language of the Church and its liturgy, an expression meaning " fallen asleep." If the marital bond is loosed in this way, she has complete freedom, even to re-marry. The group in Corinth that wanted to forbid marriage was doubly against a second marriage. In this case Paul shows himself moderate, sober, and just. And here the woman's own will alone is given as decisive. The only limitation Paul advances is to the effect that a Christian widow, if she decided on a second marriage, should only marry a man who is her brother in Christ and the Church. The less earthly need she has to marry, the stronger must be the spiritual life of the married couple. But in this case, too, the Apostle sticks with his recommendation to remain single. The word " happier " deserves special attention. It proves that he understood the greater happiness of persisting in widowhood entirely in relation to Christ, insofar as it means a greater participation in him. The widow who deliberately persists in her state of widowhood can now live again something like a second virginity and in it may bring to the service of her brothers and sisters the experiences, which are so important, of marriage and child raising.

For the last time the Apostle emphasizes that he is putting forward his personal ideas in this matter. This means that it is not a strict command, but still a claim that may venture to invoke God, the Spirit of God. Indeed it is the Spirit that expounds, in and beyond the letter, what God has revealed through

Christ and what now is to be again and again decided and lived, according to the mind of Jesus (cf. Jn. 16:13-15).

On Freedom and its Proper Use (8:1—11:1)

Among the questions from the community, there had also been the one about the way one should treat food that had been offered to idols. One must be clear that the small Christian community met with this practical question at every turn. It was not only that such food was offered for sale on the market, but Christians lived with their pagan relations or belonged to professional associations which celebrated their regular festivals with a sacrifice—rather as the medieval guilds offered a Mass for the feast of their patron saint. Ancient paganism meant something quite different from godlessness or lack of religious feeling. The whole of private and public life was consecrated to religion. How were Christians to conduct themselves at such festive meals where the connection with idolatry was certainly variously expressed but could nowhere be completely overlooked? Some were of the opinion that one should totally ignore the pagan character of the food offered, since for a Christian an idol has no real existence.

Practical Difficulties in the Use of Food Offered to Idols (8:1-13)

WHAT MUST BE THE TOUCHSTONE: KNOWLEDGE OR LOVE? (8:1-3)

[1]Now concerning food offered to idols: we know that " all of us possess knowledge." " Knowledge " puffs up, but love builds

up. ²If anyone imagines that he knows something, he does not yet know as he ought to know. ³But if one loves God, one is known by him.

Some members of the Corinthian community, probably those who set the tone, believed they had settled the problem. They took the position that since we know that idols are nothing, a dedication of food to them means nothing. Obviously, we eat it. In this attitude what is true and what is doubtful are intermingled, genuine liberation from the old worship of idols, and questionable simplification. This easily happens with sayings like " Anything goes " or " To the pure, all things are pure." Intellectuals like to invoke these liberal and avant-garde slogans. And these determined the Corinthian environment. Paul—to begin with—agrees with them. The important word, which he takes up at once, is " knowledge." We should really leave it in the original—*gnosis*—or put it between quotation marks. This word is not yet being used to describe that explicit ideology or movement which was soon to become a danger, indeed the greatest danger, to early Christianity, because the themes at work in it flowed almost indistinguishably from the center of Christianity itself and from pagan sources. The tendency which becomes apparent from this text already shows something of it. But it remains astonishing how clearly the Apostle sees the danger and how surely he touches on the weak spot.

" All of us possess knowledge." That there is " no God but one " and that therefore " an idol has no real existence " belongs to a Christian's fundamental understanding of his faith. To that extent no one need invoke it as his own and make play with this knowledge against others who have the same belief. For this is far from deciding everything. Such knowledge is no better

than the belief of the demons about which James writes in his
letter: "The demons believe—and shudder" (Jas. 2:19). If
there is a merely intellectual belief, which does not guarantee
salvation, how much more is there a knowledge which is not
as such a participation in the divine light. This reservation can
already be perceived as an undertone in the first half of the verse.
In the second it is intensified in a declaration that would have
been of annihilating sharpness for those experts in knowledge
who would have to recognize themselves as loveless. The two
effects are now radically opposed to each other! Knowledge
"puffs up" but love "builds up": on the one hand what is
ultimately empty and hollow; on the other what is not only
genuine through and through but demonstrates this genuineness
far beyond itself. We recall the "wisdom" of the first chapter.
As there human wisdom is opposed to the reality of Christ
which is divine wisdom, so here, perhaps even more sharply,
gnosis, knowledge, is opposed to *agape,* love.

"Love" is here met with for the first time in this letter
(leaving aside for the moment 4:21). We shall accept the word
and wait in patience until its entire fullness and glory are
revealed. But one thing is already clear: the building up attributed to it must be something decisive and great. If we ask,
whom does knowledge puff up, then the answer is the one
who knows, and to his own harm. Whom does love build up?
The answer is the community, and Church. Thus it brings
about what Jesus promises as the end of the mission and as
the fruit of his death: "I will build my Church" (Mt. 16:18).

"If any one imagines that he knows something . . ." Now
knowledge and love are more widely opposed to each other, in
a double sentence. Where knowledge plays the main part and
where, in order not to lag behind others, one has to say and

show as soon and as widely as possible that one has sufficient
knowledge, this is easily combined with the error, not to say
delusion, of having command of something, of having taken
hold of it. But it is precisely this being in the know that has a
habit of bearing the mark of one who has not yet come anywhere near knowing what is really to be known and understood.
For in that case he would not be so ready with his answers.
This applies absolutely to the knowledge of ultimate reality,
of God, and of divine things. A person who has been allowed
to penetrate only a little way into these has made the over-
whelming discovery that behind all knowledge new depths open
up and that what he knows slips out of his hands because it is
nothing compared with the greater thing he now begins to sense.

WHAT KNOWLEDGE KNOWS AND DOES NOT KNOW (8:4-6)

*⁴Hence, as to the eating of food offered to idols, we know that
" an idol has no real existence," and that " there is no God but
one." ⁵For although there may be so-called gods in heaven or on
earth—as indeed there are many " gods " and many " lords "—
⁶yet for us there is one God, the Father, from whom are all
things and for whom we exist, and one Lord, Jesus Christ,
through whom are all things and through whom we exist.*

It was part of the hasty temperament and spiritual force of the
Apostle Paul at once to apply the highest standards and to open
up the ultimate horizons of any question. He has just done this
here. But he knows that not all can keep up with him. So he
now sets out to approach the problem one step at a time. For
this purpose he puts the question again quite openly and then
fills in, step by step, somewhat more concretely, what belongs

to " knowledge " in this matter. The second half of the sentence
is completely clear : " There is no God but one." The first half
is harder to define. Does Paul want to say that idols do not exist?
The next verse would contradict that. Does he want to say that
idols do indeed exist, but that they are nothing? That does not
fit in so well with the addition " on earth." A certain impression
arises perhaps from the fact that the word for idol (*eidolon*)
means in the first case an image, while the next verse speaks
simply of " gods." It is they to whom the religion of antiquity
attributed a field of authority " in heaven " or " on earth."
Paul says of them explicitly that many really exist, insofar as
men submit themselves to such conceptions and thus lend them
reality. The " lords " (*kyrioi*) who were honored as gods may
well lead us to think of the cult of the ruler making its way
from East to West.

Further, it is here, for the first time in the New Testament,
that the role of co-creator is assigned to Christ Jesus, and this in
a form that does not seem in any way like a private speculation
but sounds much more like a communal profession.

WHAT LOVE DOES (8:7–13)

*[7]However, not all possess this knowledge. But some, through
being hitherto accustomed to idols, eat food as really offered to
an idol; and their conscience, being weak, is defiled. [8]Food will
not commend us to God. We are no worse off if we do not eat,
and no better off if we do. [9]Only take care lest this liberty of
yours somehow become a stumbling block to the weak. [10]For if
anyone sees you, a man of knowledge, at table in an idol's
temple, might he not be encouraged, if his conscience is weak, to
eat food offered to idols? [11]And so by your knowledge this weak*

*man is destroyed, the brother for whom Christ died. [12]Thus,
sinning against your brethren and wounding their conscience
when it is weak, you sin against Christ. [13]Therefore, if food
is a cause of my brother's falling, I will never eat meat, lest I
cause my brother to fall.*

In the middle of the 50's the Corinthian faithful were marked,
in their attitudes and habits, by a few years of Christianity but
by generations of paganism. It required long reflection to see
food served at such meals not as sacred but as profane. Some certainly tried, more or less voluntarily, to do as the more advanced, but they did not catch up so quickly and felt burdened
in conscience, while others perhaps made it their particular mission to press on with emancipation and to eat ostentatiously, as
if it were a question of gaining a victory for God's cause in this
way. Paul remains cool towards these last. Eating will not give
us an increase of grace, and if we do not eat, we are no worse
off. Properly understood, eating can do either, but for this
it is necessary to perceive the decisive motives and occasions.

For the situation cannot be overlooked which Paul describes
with the word " weak." This key word is repeated four times.
It means uncertainty and anxiety of conscience. The other group
can be described by the word here translated as " liberty," which
can, however, also be translated as " right " or " authority." This
liberty is in danger of turning into heedlessness, which could
injure the weak or cause them to fall. Should the weak be
destroyed through another's knowledge? Should the man who
feels and behaves in such a superior way say perhaps " Then it
serves him right "? May one speak like this if one knows one
self to be redeemed by Christ? Do we not all live because account was taken of us when we were still weak (cf. Rom. 5:6)?

Truly we no longer deserve the grace of Christ, indeed we sin against Christ himself if we neglect this concern for others. These others are our brothers in Christ and, to put it yet more personally, each one is " my brother." By dying for him as for me, Christ made him my brother, and we can only attain salvation with one another, as brothers. Towards the end of the chapter Paul sums up all his arguments unmistakably in this title of " brother." He can still appeal to the newly felt experience of brotherhood in the young community, but even this young community already needs to be shown the obligation brotherhood involves. The " strong " need this. They are not here described like this as they are in the many respects parallel section of the letter to the Romans (15 : 1ff.). But it is quite unmistakable that precisely because of what makes them strong, they have a duty to take greater care of the others. Although Paul can certainly reckon himself among the strong, so far as knowledge and freedom and authority are concerned, he shows clearly his special love for the weak. However much he may do justice to the advanced thinkers on the question of knowledge, in his heart he is much closer to those who cannot so quickly shake off all scruples.

The Example of the Apostle in Limiting His Own Freedom
(9:1-27)

THE CORINTHIANS SEEM TO HAVE UNDERSTOOD THE APOSTLE'S CONDUCT BADLY, OR EVEN TO HAVE MISUNDERSTOOD IT ALTOGETHER (9:1-6)

¹Am I not free? Am I not an apostle? Have I not seen Jesus our Lord? Are not you my workmanship in the Lord? ²If to others I am not an apostle, at least I am to you; for you are the seal of my apostleship in the Lord. ³This is my defense to those who would examine me. ⁴Do we not have the right to our food and drink? ⁵Do we not have the right to be accompanied by a wife, as the other apostles and the brethren of the Lord and Cephas? ⁶Or is it only Barnabas and I who have the right to refrain from working for a living?

The people who gave themselves so much credit for their " knowledge " are the same who set such store by their freedom, as has already been intimated (6: 12–20). Now the subject of freedom is developed more explicitly. The reference to freedom or liberty is repeated in 9: 19 and 10: 29. In essence Paul shows that the freedom of the Christian is a great good, but not the only one, and not the highest. There are reasons for renouncing the use of freedom. This is ultimately not the opposite of freedom but true freedom.

Combined with this theme of freedom, which the Apostle wants to illustrate by his own example, is a necessary *apologia pro vita sua,* a self-defense. It would have been part of his freedom to have himself maintained as an Apostle by the missionary communities of that time. He had his special reasons for not making use of this right. But there were people who only saw in this a confirmation that he was not a full apostle. All the days of his life he had to suffer from the fact that he did not belong to the original apostles who had known the Lord in Galilee and Jerusalem.

Yet if in his calling to the apostolic office Paul stands in a certain measure on his own, while the twelve could give mutual testimony to their calling, there was still, for the Corinthians, another proof—the existence of their community. No one can

dispute his foundation of this community, which had already become important. The concept of Apostle comprised, so to say,
two aspects: on the one side, he is the representative of Jesus;
on the other, he is a founder of churches. The two belong
together, but the one must show itself in the other. To that
extent the existence of the Corinthian community is the seal that
the Lord himself has impressed on Paul's mission. Not the only
one, but this one may suffice for the Corinthians.

In a way this was already a reply, a rejection, and justification
in face of certain hostile manifestations and detractions. But perhaps verse 3 relates still more to the following sentences which,
in the form of rhetorical questions, enumerate one by one the
rights he had as an Apostle. They give us evidence of facts very
interesting for Church history, though not without leaving individual questions open: "Do we not have the *exousia?*" In
this Greek concept the elements of freedom, full powers, and
rights combine. Immediately in question is the right to support
by the community that falls to an apostle, and not only to himself but also to the wife accompanying him. So it was with " the
other apostles and the brethren of the Lord and Cephas." We
know who Cephas is. Who the brethren of the Lord are cannot be exactly determined. The brothers of the Lord, James
and Joses (Mk. 15:40), have this honorary title in the primitive
Church, but their more precise relationship has not been made
plain with certainty. Also included are Simon and Judas (Mk.
6:3) who were probably the sons of Cleophas, a brother of
Joseph. One can understand that anyone who could in any way
lay claim to this title would be glad to do so.

However, the question of the " wife " is also of interest here.
If wives are described as " sisters," this means that, as Christians,
they are members of the Church. Most probable is the assumption

that it is a question of the wives of married apostles. It is true
that they were once asked to leave everything. But there is strong
evidence that this command was confined to that period when
they first followed Jesus.

THE RIGHTS OF AN APOSTLE CORRESPOND TO A GENERAL HUMAN AND EVEN DIVINE LAW (9:7-10)

*⁷Who serves as a soldier at his own expense? Who plants a vine-
yard without eating any of its fruit? Who tends a flock without
getting some of the milk? ⁸Do I say this on human authority?
Does not the law say the same? ⁹For it is written in the law of
Moses, " You shall not muzzle an ox when it is treading out the
grain." Is it for oxen that God is concerned? ¹⁰Does he not speak
entirely for our sake? It was written for our sake, because the
ploughman should plough in hope and the thresher thresh in
hope of a share in the crop.*

Paul reinforces with these expressive comparisons the right
obtaining in the primitive Church, in which we see an early
form of ecclesiastical tax. The apostolic calling has something
of all three in it: of military service—" a good soldier of Christ
Jesus " (2 Tim. 2:3); of work in a vineyard (cf. 3:6; Mt.
20:1-16); and of the tending of flocks (cf. Acts 20:28). In all
three callings it is understood that the man who serves in them
should also live from them. This belongs, if one may say so,
to the unwritten but everywhere valid natural law. But in a
matter that extends so far into the spiritual, Paul does not want
to rest simply on arguments of sound human sense.

He adds a spiritual argument that of course, strictly speaking, is only a comparison (at least the first one is; a more compelling one follows in verse 14). Is there a little humor at work when Paul brings in this " humane " concern for the ox treading out the grain? In any case, it is a very thoughtful trait in the Mosaic law to think of the position of animals who, in threshing, have stubble and ears constantly before their eyes and in their nose, and it would be decidedly hard to deprive them of every opportunity of taking an occasional mouthful.

THEY ARE COMPLETELY APPROPRIATE TO THE SPIRITUAL FIELD (9:11–14)

[11]*If we have sown spiritual good among you, is it too much if we reap your material benefits?* [12]*If others share this rightful claim among you, do not we still more? Nevertheless, we have not made use of this right, but we endure anything rather than put an obstacle in the way of the gospel of Christ.* [13]*Do you not know that those who are employed in the temple service get their food from the temple, and those who serve at the altar share in the sacrificial offerings?* [14]*In the same way, the Lord commanded that those who proclaim the gospel should get their living by the gospel.*

It would be quite misplaced if someone were to object that this rule cannot apply in the spiritual field. Paul established, with even more right on his side, that what a community offers its missionary or pastor can always only be slight in relation to what it receives from him, for the spiritual is basically always more than the secular. Paul actually uses the word " material " meaning " fleshly." Clearly for the Corinthians nothing was too much for their newest favorites. This refers to those preachers who had so much impressed them with their " loftier " manner of preaching. The sarcastic observation of 2 Corinthians 11 : 20 puts their captivating manner in a still sharper light.

Now at last Paul says why he and his fellow workers have made and wish to make no use of this right, so emphatically proclaimed. He wants to avoid the slightest appearance of caring whether he lived well at the expense of the gospel. Nevertheless, he again takes up the position in law, as it is provided for by pagans and Jews alike, that their priests live by the service of the temple, by the altar. The way of life of the Mediterranean lands was essentially agrarian, and their economy a natural economy. So the offerings in the temple and to the gods were at the same time the given form of Church tax and payment for the priests. But it is significant that at this point Paul also brings in an explicit command of Jesus as the ultimate and conclusive argument. It is true that he does not cite any saying of the Lord, but rather assumes it to be known. But what tradition has preserved (Mt. 10 : 10; Lk. 10 : 7) could be the wording intended here. We should take this into consideration in two ways. On the one hand, the services of the gospel can be simply compared with what was formerly the cult of God or the gods. On the other, the priesthood of the New Testament may not fall back into the conception of itself held by the Old Testament or even the pagan priesthood.

Nevertheless, Paul Has Made No Use of Them (9:15–18)

¹⁵*But I have made no use of any of these rights, nor am I writing this to secure any such provision. For I would rather die than*

have anyone deprive me of my ground for boasting. ¹⁶For if I preach the gospel, that gives me no ground for boasting. For necessity is laid upon me. Woe to me if I do not preach the gospel! ¹⁷For if I do this of my own will, I have a reward; but if not of my own will, I am entrusted with a commission. ¹⁸What then is my reward? Just this: that in my preaching I may make the gospel free of charge, not making full use of my right in the gospel.

It is painful for Paul to expose his conduct and motives in this way, all the more as he now has to fear that people in Corinth might begin to feel ashamed over what they had so thoughtlessly accepted, just as children thoughtlessly accept the greatest sacrifices made by their parents. And then their pride could no longer endure that the Apostle of such a rich community should not be supported by it. That he most resolutely refuses. One notes his excitement in the fevered construction of the sentence, which is not lost in translation. In such passages one seems to detect, even to hear, how the Apostle's temperament affected the dictation of his letters.

But why is he so set upon this exception? He had already given one reason (9:12). He now allows another more personal one to be forced from him, for clearly he has been touched very deeply—hence the present outbreak. It again fits in with the special character of his calling. To proclaim the gospel like the others is too little for one who had once wanted to destroy the Church. Since Christ had overpowered him by the revelation of his own self, Paul felt himself under an obligation, delivered over, and pledged to Christ, to a degree that far exceeded any possible measure. He pushes it, or it pushes him, to the word " necessity," though naturally he cannot mean to say that he is not acting from the freest of will and with his whole heart. But it is precisely this that he feels to be the one thing that is right, so that he cannot do other than give over his entire freedom to it. Between the freedom, with which this whole chapter is concerned, and this necessity, there exists an inner connection. Whatever the word " necessity " may mean, it is clear that Paul does not mean here the opposite of freedom. On the contrary, freedom is fulfilled in this necessity, the innermost core of freedom is that necessity with which a man fully recognizes what is worthy of his whole power of loving and giving, when, ultimately, he loves God.

Do not men also experience in human love the oneness of freedom and necessity? In Christ is reflected the same mystery in the oneness of the obedience and love of the Son. He can speak of the necessity that is laid upon him. But he affirms it fully and totally, as truly as he knows himself to be the Son. Insofar as we are men—and Jesus too belongs to us according to his created humanity—such necessity comes upon us from without because he who demands, calls, sends, and claims stands over against us. But as soon as this claim upon men is totally accepted by them—and with us this happens in faith and love— it ceases to be a necessity from without. Paul's " woe to me " does not indicate a threat from without but one that is actually worse—from within. The man would be torn within himself. It sounds almost unbearable when Paul says that he preaches the gospel " not of his own will." But we understand what he wants to say. And it is still more important if we detect what drives him to such daring statements. For the truth here is less in concepts that can be weighed upon scales than in impulses from the innermost heart that burst all bonds, as it is the true measure of love to be measureless.

" What then is my reward?" he asks. Do not the words
" reward " and " ground for boasting," which, incidentally, are
repeated (9: 15-18), call forth a painful impression? Is it not ego-
istical and self-interested? Reputation, the " ground for boasting," for the men of antiquity, or rather for biblical man,
and in any case for Paul, was not something as external as it has
become for us. Reputation is in the first instance the inner
witness of a good conscience. That he preaches the gospel gives
him no ground for giving himself credit. In this there is nothing
in which he could make sure of his unreserved obedience and
total self-giving, and nothing, therefore, that merits reward. That
he hopes for a reward is as obvious as that he hopes for eternal
life. For the reward is God himself. And any kind of calculation
is far removed from this hope. Only in this way would the idea
of reward be debased. Though the motive of reward may have
played an undesirable role in a certain type of piety, the
Christian of today should not fall into the opposite extreme, as
if any thought of reward were unworthy of a human being. That
would mean man setting himself above the whole New Testament, above the preaching of Jesus and of the Apostles. Not to
be in the least interested in reward would be pride, would
destroy the basic relationship of man to God, and would mean
rejecting not only his reward but also his grace.

... IN THE FIRST PLACE FOR PASTORAL REASONS (9:19-22)

*19For though I am free from all men, I have made myself a slave
to all, that I might win the more. 20To the Jews I became as a
Jew, in order to win Jews; to those under the law I became as
one under the law—though not being myself under the law—that*

I might win those under the law. ²¹To those outside the law I became as one outside the law—not being without law toward God but under the law of Christ—that I might win those outside the law. ²²To the weak I became weak, that I might win the weak. I have become all things to all men, that I might by all means save some.

The line of thought of the whole of these three chapters ranges very far, but it also binds the threads into a firm net. Paul has not forgotten that he invoked the Christian understanding of freedom in his practical ruling on the attitude towards sacrificial food. As a protection against misuse by the self-consciously strong, he goes on to consider his own way of life in this light. That he renounces his right to payment is only a part of his total behavior. He presents the antithesis impressively: " free for all men—a slave to all." This is his freely chosen rule of life.

When Paul holds to the sabbath here, but not there, here undertakes circumcision, there forbids it, such conduct could be understood as indecisiveness or, by the ill-disposed, as an accommodation to circumstances through weakness of character. But nothing could be more unjust. In all this there was neither arbitrariness nor whim. He knows he is bound by an invisible law. One could not describe it more briefly and define it more comprehensively than Paul does here. He calls it " the law of Christ." What he gathers together in this most densely packed expression contains not only the example of Christ, who stood above the sabbath and yet submitted himself to this law, but above all the Spirit of Christ which ever anew points to and makes actual the example of Christ. A person who does not understand his freedom in Christ as being also the law of Christ has understood nothing.

" All things to all men " is one of the Apostle's bold phrases. He could venture it. But who outside the ranks of the greatest saints can lay claim to it if it is taken seriously, even in the sense of an attempt? Paul did not mean to justify it by a hectic activity, taking pleasure in ceaseless effort. We must not forget for a moment the objective towards which all this is tending—the concern for the weak that comes so hard to the strong. Weak though they may be, at any rate in the eyes of men, they have their rights before God and with them their rights in the Church, as truly as the Son of God chose the little ones and hailed the poor as blessed.

". . . that I might by all means save some." It would actually have been appropriate to add to the universalist " all things to all men " the words: " that I might save all." He would perhaps have had the same right to say it. But he refrains from doing so. He only allows himself to say " that I might by all means save some," that is, some in any case. He knows that it will never be all and the Church must also know that she cannot reach, let alone win, or save, all. It is something else again that the assembly of the few also means something for the rest, on account of the primary law of the economy of salvation, that some represent others. This law the Second Vatican Council pronounced in the fundamental declaration that the Church is " the sacrament of the salvation for mankind "—no more and no less.

. . . But Also so as Not to Risk His Own Salvation (9:23–27)

[23]*I do all for the sake of the gospel, that I may share in its blessings. [24]Do you not know that in a race all the runners compete,*

but only one receives the prize? So run that you may obtain it.
[25]Every athlete exercises self-control in all things. They do it to
receive a perishable wreath, but we an imperishable. [26]Well, I do
not run aimlessly, I do not box as one beating the air; [27]but I
pommel my body and subdue it, lest after preaching to others I
myself should be disqualified.

In the train of this sweeping " all " the next verse leads on to
another crucial point. " All for the sake of the gospel ": that
could sum up once again what has gone before. But now it is no
longer to win others but " that I may share in its blessings."
What a surprising development. The Apostle has to be concerned not only for the spiritual health of others, but also for his
own. (The real point of the thought remains unexpressed : If I,
how much more you!) It is not possible for a man, even if he be
an Apostle, to be so certain of his own salvation that he need
devote himself to the salvation of others only from a position of
safety of his own. One's own election is, it is true, a precondition
for service to one's brethren, but this again is a presupposition
for the other. In this consists the ultimate solidarity of all in the
Church, which binds at the deepest level those who teach and
minister to those who hear and receive. This distinction is indeed
rather widely applicable but it does not extend into the inner
mystery of holiness and grace. There the distinction becomes
superfluous and ministering and receiving can even be reversed.

Somehow the Apostle seems to have been touched for a
moment by the thought of other nugatory goals for which men
strive, as when a man runs aimlessly to and fro or—and now
the Apostle changes to another kind of sport—like a boxer who
strikes the air. But who is the opponent Paul wants to beat
down? His own body! So Christianity is, after all, hostile to the

body? One must be clear that a double image is used here. Paul sees the danger of the Corinthians, who were in process of making Christianity easy for themselves, forgetting that following Jesus means fighting with the world and against one's own self. But since he is already pursuing the image of the boxing match, the opponent also has to be presented pictorially. Doubtless he means by this harsh expression, which in modern boxing terminology might be equivalent to a hook to the chin, not ascetic exercises or chastisements but those austerities and hardships that life as an apostle imposed on him, and which he demanded ruthlessly of himself. The point is the same as in verse 19: " I have made myself a slave to all." The sharper note comes from the fact that he wants to make the Corinthians aware with the greatest possible emphasis of the dangerous game they are playing. If he, the Apostle, can still be afraid of being found unworthy of the prize and being disqualified as a failure, how much more will they have reason to be on their guard against themselves.

Warning Examples from the History of Israel of a False Assurance of Salvation (10:1–13)

The Sacraments Do Not Guarantee Salvation ... (10:1-5)

¹*I want you to know, brethren, that our fathers were all under the cloud, and all passed through the sea, ²and all were baptized into Moses in the cloud and in the sea, ³and all ate the same supernatural food ⁴and all drank the same supernatural drink. For they drank from the supernatural Rock which followed*

*them, and the Rock was Christ. ⁵Nevertheless, with most of them
God was not pleased; for they were overthrown in the wilder-
ness.*

In the events that Paul cites here, has he not taken something
from out of the fullness of the Old Testament texts? One might
perhaps think of the example of the ox treading out the grain,
though what he brings in here is on another level. Why? These
examples stem from the time of Israel's wanderings in the desert.
After being led out of Egypt, the enduring symbol of salvation,
the people of God were on their way to the promised land, the
enduring symbol of fulfillment. Between the two lies this strange
period that is full of marvels and proofs of God's love, so that
later it could be celebrated and almost idealized as the time of
young love between God and his people though it was also a
period full of backsliding, grumbling, and rejection as well, so
that it can also appear as one single chain of sins (as in some
of the psalms). This is not by chance. In this period the entire
ambiguity of all human history can be seen.

That is why Paul can call the Israelites " our fathers," even
though the Corinthians were for the greater part not Jews. They
are our fathers because there is only one saving history within
which God continually advances salvation and upholds certain
structures. One such structure is the sacramental one. When
Paul says that they were baptized and ate and drank, this is at
first surprising for us. Is he not carrying back the Christian
sacraments to a time when they did not yet exist? He too knows
that Christian baptism and the Christian eucharist did not yet
exist at that time. But he also knows the opposite—that Christian
baptism and the Christian eucharist trace their roots back there
and are prefigured there. What was granted to them there was

for them equivalently and according to the circumstances the same as falls to our lot in baptism and eucharist. It is precisely this that makes saving history one.

This text, moreover, recognizes for the first time that baptism and eucharist belong together. In itself there was no occasion to speak of baptism here if the Apostle had not already known both as spiritual events of a in some ways similar type, that is as " sacraments." It would have been hard for Paul to have found, or even to have merely looked for, the Old Testament equivalent to baptism, if this had not already been to hand in the correspondence between the eucharist and manna. But it is immediately understandable with Paul presupposing baptism by total immersion (probably also in running water) that the passage through the water, i.e. salvation by water, can be compared with baptism. What then is the meaning of the cloud? Is it meant here as an element linked to the water, or an element in its own right, insofar as it points to God's effective presence? The cloud is in any case again and again the grace-giving manifestation of the Lord of the covenant. But both water and cloud first became quasi-sacramental signs through Moses. " Baptized into Moses " probably means, as informed by anticipation of the Christian reality, that the Israelites, by attachment in faith to Moses, became sharers in his grace-given relationship to God, as we do through baptism " into Christ Jesus " (Rom. 6 : 3).

. . . FOR THOSE WHO CHALLENGE THE LORD (10:6–11)

⁶Now these things are warnings for us, not to desire evil as they did. ⁷Do not be idolaters as some of them were; as it is written, " The people sat down to eat and drink and rose up to dance."

⁸We must not indulge in immorality as some of them did, and twenty-three thousand fell in a single day. ⁹We must not put the Lord to the test, as some of them did and were destroyed by serpents; ¹⁰nor grumble, as some of them did and were destroyed by the Destroyer. ¹¹Now these things happened to them as a warning, but they were written down for our instruction, upon whom the end of the ages has come.

As God's saving work becomes greater, the responsibility and danger for the human partner in the covenant mount also. The Old Testament has already contrasted with God's saving activity the ungrateful and wicked behavior of the elect, the recipients of God's grace. They desired or lusted, they became idolaters, they indulged in immorality. In practice all three sins ran together. The pagan cult attracted them on account of its joy in the senses and its sensuality. The Israelites would always have liked to introduce into the cult of Yahweh such permissive, orgiastic festivals. Often they did not want actually to desert Yahweh but merely to honor him as the Gentiles honored their gods.

But God Is Faithful to Those Who Truly Hope in Him (10:12–13)

¹²Therefore let anyone who thinks that he stands take heed lest he fall. ¹³No temptation has overtaken you that is not common to man. God is faithful, and he will not let you be tempted beyond your strength, but with the temptation will also provide the way of escape, that you may be able to endure it.

What makes one fear most for the Corinthians is their self-assurance. They behave and feel as if for them there were no more danger. They allow themselves liberties as if they already possessed their salvation. Certainly in a sense faith and the sacraments make future salvation already present. But no believer is exempt from that essential mark of human existence that we know as the pilgrim state. So long as a man lives, there is always as much reason to hope as there is to fear. The man who excludes one of these two commits one of the gravest sins. It is not as if a believer should not think of himself as being in grace. But as he thinks and rejoices in this, he must at the same time think too that he could lose it, and that more quickly than he at that moment would consider possible. No one stands in such a way that he could not also fall. And the Apostle puts it even more carefully: " Let any one who thinks that he stands take heed . . ."

Practical Decisions on the Question of Food Offered in Sacrifice (10:14—11:1)

EITHER: PARTICIPATION IN THE BODY OF CHRIST (10:14-17)

[14]*Therefore, my beloved, shun the worship of idols.* [15]*I speak as to sensible men; judge for yourselves what I say.* [16]*The cup of blessing which we bless, is it not a participation in the blood of Christ? The bread which we break, is it not a participation in the body of Christ?* [17]*Because there is one bread, we who are many are one body, for we all partake of the one bread.*

These verses are of the very greatest significance for us in several respects. From them we receive precious information on the central mystery of the Church, the celebration and understanding of the eucharist. One does not know whether to be more surprised that in all the other writings of the New Testament we learn scarcely anything about it, or simply grateful that in this letter at least we are given such important testimony. We shall try to weigh every word with the greatest care and to savor every nuance in these two verses that embrace the eucharistic mystery of the Church.

" The cup of blessing ": we have here a well-established expression derived from Judaism. It seems the most solemn point in the Paschal meal. During the ritual meal lasting several hours, the cup was passed around four times. The third of these was the most important because over it the head of the household, as president of the assembled company, spoke the solemn prayer of thanksgiving or blessing. It was therefore crowned with a wreath. In later times other celebrations were similarly concluded with a prayer of thanksgiving and a " cup of blessing." If Paul here assumes this idea to be familiar, it is a sure indication that the primitive Church had already made this expression her own, within and without Palestine, to describe her eucharist.

" Which we bless ": why this repetition? Perhaps to dis- tinguish the Christian cup from the Jewish and perhaps also from any Gentile cup? We cannot be sure of seeing here a play on the words of consecration. Nevertheless, this short sentence means in practice nothing else and nothing less than the euchar- istic prayer of the Church with which she does, for her part, what the Lord did, " giving thanks (blessing)."

" Is it not a participation in the blood of Christ? " The con- tents of the cup have become the blood of Christ through the act of eucharistic blessing. This cup is participation in the blood of Christ for all who drink of it. Perhaps one can say further, common participation : community with someone through par-

ticipation in something. Many translations give the meaning of
" fellowship in the body of Christ." As much as one would like
today to give priority to the concept of fellowship, on account
of its personal content, this does not combine well logically with
" the blood of Christ." It does of course remain true that through
drinking the blood of Christ fellowship with Christ is brought
about. But what is first present here and what happens sacra-
mentally, that is visibly, is this participation in something. For
Paul the spiritual and personal was so obvious that he does not
consider it necessary to emphasize it.

" The bread which we break, is it not a participation in the
blood of Christ? " This sentence is unmistakably built exactly
parallel to the preceding one. " Breaking bread " is originally
in no way exclusively a description of the eucharistic meal. But
the parallelism seems already to indicate such a development.
But why does the sentence about the cup come first? Probably
because the main argument fits in better with what Paul has to
say about bread.

" Because there is one bread, we who are many are one body."
A surprising twist! Bread and body were being discussed, the
bread that in the eucharistic celebration becomes the body of
Christ. Now the body suddenly becomes another body, or rather
it emerges that through this celebration Christ not only receives
a body in the form of bread but also a body in the form of
the community, the Church. Indeed, the body's form as
bread actually exists to make the Church real and visible as
Christ's body. The two meanings and realities of the body meet
in the eucharistic event in which, through the breaking of the
one bread, the many not only receive their share but in receiving
this share become again in a mysterious manner the whole, the
body of Christ.

Or: Partnership with Demons (10:18–22)

[18]Consider the practice of Israel; are not those who eat the sacrifices partners in the altar? [19]What do I imply then? That food offered to idols is anything, or that an idol is anything? [20]No, I imply that what pagans sacrifice they offer to demons and not to God. I do not want you to be partners with demons. [21]You cannot drink the cup of the Lord and the cup of demons. You cannot partake of the table of the Lord and the table of demons. [22]Shall we provoke the Lord to jealousy? Are we stronger than he?

The fellowship of the eucharistic meal signifies and effects through body and blood an inner union with the living Lord. We have been brought up from childhood on this idea and have seen the uniqueness and incomparability of what we called then, and still call today, holy communion. As children we were less able to see that there was something like communion for Jews too and even for pagans. With the powerful emphasis on the change in the bread and wine, there was no possibility of our understanding that in sacrifice as understood by all peoples, a kind of transformation occurred in their offering too. The dedication to the godhead became effective, in a manner both real and symbolic, through the sacrificial fire of the altar. The fire, which in the understanding of a man receptive to archetypal data sprang from the heavens, did not so much devour the sacrificial food as transform it. The man who ate this food which was filled with power of the godhead became united to the godhead itself. Wherever the sacrifice was offered, those who offered it were convinced that by participation in the sacrificial meal— and this was almost always a fixed part of the sacrifice—they became guests of the divine and receivers of divine gifts.

The train of thought is concluded with a rhetorical question taken from the context of the song of Moses (Deut. 32:21), already touched on above. The question " Are we stronger than he? " makes it once again clear to whom the whole argument is primarily directed: the strong ones of Corinth.

WHAT CAN BE SAID IN PRIVATE CASES (10:23–30)

[23]"*All things are lawful," but not all things are helpful. "All things are lawful," but not all things build up.* [24]*Let no one seek his own good, but the good of his neighbor.* [25]*Eat whatever is sold in the meat market without raising any question on the ground of conscience.* [26]*For " the earth is the Lord's, and everything in it."* [27]*If one of the unbelievers invites you to dinner and you are disposed to go, eat whatever is set before you without raising any question on the ground of conscience.* [28](*But if some one says to you, " This has been offered in sacrifice," then out of consideration for the man who informed you, and for conscience's sake—*[29]*I mean his conscience, not yours—do not eat it.) For why should my liberty be determined by another man's scruples?* [30]*If I partake with thankfulness, why am I denounced because of that for which I give thanks?*

Now that he has warded off the danger that people in Corinth would misinterpret and falsify his doctrine of freedom, Paul can finally come to the point of laying down the practical instructions which follow from these basic principles. He expressly brings up three cases, though not without recalling yet again a principle that he has already impressed on them in an earlier context (6:12). It can do no harm for them to see how the same fundamental ideas apply in this matter also.

The first case is quite straightforward. What is sold on the market can be bought and eaten without further thought. Here any appearance of idolatry is excluded. The second case is somewhat more personal: an invitation from an unbeliever. Here too there applies a fundamental freedom. But there can also, and this makes the third case, be need for a restriction. If someone points out, probably an anxious Christian who is a fellow guest, that it is sacrificial meat, then concern for the weak must prevail.

Verses 29 and 30 are difficult. Who is speaking here? Is Paul here giving us the words of an objector? That would make good sense of the main wording. But neither the introductory " for " nor what follows as an answer in verse 31 will fit properly. So it is better to see Paul's own thought in it. He is then saying: If you abstain out of consideration for the other, then above all you are not condemned by the other's conscience. He cannot think you are a bad Christian. In the same way, a healthy man can eat what a sick man perhaps cannot, but the healthy man does not become sick if he goes without this food.

WHAT APPLIES TO ALL CASES AND IN THE LAST ANALYSIS (10:31—11:1)

[31]*So, whether you eat or drink, or whatever you do, do all to the glory of God.* [32]*Give no offense to Jews or to Greeks or to the church of God,* [33]*just as I try to please all men in everything I do, not seeking my own advantage, but that of many, that they may be saved.* [1]*Be imitators of me, as I am of Christ.*

Paul by no means wishes to confine himself to casuistic individual rulings. He has to bring the whole issue once more into its wider context, and raise it to the heights. It may be a question of the eating of certain food, but he extends the question to what he regards as essential for a Christian—to all eating and drinking, and even to every action and activity. Thus he by no means confines himself to religious acts. To a Christian everything whatever is related to God, and everything whatever a Christian does can glorify God. The man who eats or drinks, who does what belongs to human existence, who makes use of the things of the world which the Creator has intended for man, he will everywhere come upon God and will therefore again and again expressly thank God for it. It will be a cause of deepest rejoicing to him to remember that in this way he is fulfilling the highest objective that he can wish for in life: giving glory to God.

A twofold thought finally concludes this theme. First there is a warning once again to avoid offense on all sides and to take an example of this from him. And then, as a complete surprise, comes the reference to the example of Christ.

On Conduct in the Liturgical Assembly (11:2–34)

After dealing with the question of sacrificial food, in which an important area of intercourse between Christians and their pagan environment is clarified, the letter turns again to the internal problems of the community. There are really three of these: 1) the veiling of women in the communal assembly; 2) the proper form of the eucharistic celebration; 3) the proper ranking of the gifts of the Spirit. The third, however, on account of its extent over three chapters, we shall ourselves treat in a separate chapter.

The Veiling of Women in the Communal Assembly (11:2–16)

THE MORE GENERAL THEOLOGICAL AND HUMAN ARGUMENTS (11:2–6)

²I commend you because you remember me in everything and maintain the traditions even as I have delivered them to you. ³But I want you to understand that the head of every man is Christ, the head of a woman is her husband, and the head of Christ is God. ⁴Any man who prays or prophesies with his head covered dishonors his head, ⁵but any woman who prays or prophesies with her head unveiled dishonors her head—it is the same as if her head were shaven. ⁶For if a woman will not veil herself, then she should cut off her hair; but if it is disgraceful for a woman to be shorn or shaven, let her wear a veil.

Before each reply to a concrete question, a basic theological order is set up. In this Paul again shows that as a theologian he prefers to proceed from the loftiest principles, even when it is a question of very mundane things, like this question of whether women should wear veils on their heads at church services or not. " Praying " and " prophesying " refer to proceedings in the communal assembly. There was no question that at such assemblies women might speak, in the same way as men. But this evidently did not satisfy some women. They wanted to speak like the men, with head uncovered. In itself such speaking in public, in the community, was already a significant step beyond Greek, let alone Jewish custom. It was the consequence of that essential equality of the sexes in Christ (Gal. 3:28), founded by him and expressed in several ways by Paul. Because, however, " all things are lawful for me " could be misunderstood in a city like Corinth, in the sense of laxity, indeed of libertinism, Paul has to pull vigorously on the brake. In present-day Judaism a man must cover his head when he enters the synagogue. This was not the case in St. Paul's time. Nor, however, does he require of women such a total veiling as has been practiced by the Eastern Islamic peoples up to our own time. He is really trying to be a Jew to the Jews and a Greek to the Greeks. What he wants to prevent is falsification of the gospel.

The line of thought starts with a kind of " head " theology. " The head of every man is Christ . . ." We feel at once that the word " head " carries with it ideas that are no longer current among us, inasmuch as we cannot equate them with another that is all too prevalent, as if " head " were the same as " sovereign." " Head " certainly means that one thing is " over " another, but in an order of mutual belonging. This is most decisively expressed in the last link in the chain : " and the head of Christ is God." High as Christ stands, so that he has a name that is over all names, and in this name every knee bows in heaven, on earth, and under the earth, there remains a clear order. This name Christ received. God gave it to him. And this remains in full force, even when the name means equality with God. If this applies in the first place to the incarnate one, in another way it applies too to the second divine Person. The Son is indeed of the same substance as the Father, but he has this substance from the Father : God from God, light from light. The Father remains the origin, even in the Trinity, and for the New Testament revelation too, he remains simply " God." This is important for all the other links in Paul's chain of argument. Being the head includes being above as well as belonging together, in a living, substantive relationship that makes life possible precisely by containing a clear order. Order means superior and inferior. Paul is here speaking within the context of revelation in the realm of grace. There may be, outside Christianity, a subordination of the woman to the man, which goes so far here as to be reflected in Christian custom. But this is to be measured against the order of grace as given in revelation. Only thus can the good that is in it prove itself and become itself a means of grace by being taken up into this order of grace. Of course, to attain the order of grace one must open oneself to the spirit of Jesus who did not come to be served but to serve.

BIBLICAL CONSIDERATIONS (11:7–12)

[7]*For a man ought not to cover his head, since he is the image and glory of God; but woman is the glory of man.* [8]*(For man was not made from woman, but woman from man.* [9]*Neither was man created for woman, but woman for man.)* [10]*That is why a woman ought to have a veil on her head, because of the angels.* [11]*(Nevertheless, in the Lord woman is not independent of man nor man of woman;* [12]*for as woman was made from man, so man is now born of woman. And all things are from God.)*

Paul takes up his train of thought with the man and tries to establish why it is that he should not cover his head. The image of God should be visible in him. The woman also shares in this dignity, but through her relation to the man: she is the " glory of man " if she is what she should be. Behind this ranking can be seen the creation story, the so-called second creation story. There it is related how the woman was created for the man, as is said yet more plainly in the next two verses. This stirs up many people today who accept the equal rights of woman, and seems intolerable to them. But it is very much a question of how one reads such a text. It does not mean that the man is created for his own sake. If one puts this question, then one would have to answer that the man is created for the world, for the practical world and its practical administration. But the woman is created for the man, for personal values. In this way the sexes complement each other. We have now learned, however, that the woman too can take over the practical tasks that were previously only allotted to the man. Nevertheless, the woman must have the time and strength to be and to give what she and only she has to be and to give to the man, the family, civilization, and the world.

Understanding verse 10 involves two questions. What is the meaning of what the woman should have on her head? Is it a sign of subordination to the man or perhaps of the authority of the man, as in marriage? This ordering of the sexes, which is aimed above all at the clear recognition of the married and unmarried states and their distinction from each other, in the case of the Christian community is not only humanly justified but also " because of the angels." Angels have their part in the divine worship of the Church—let us remember the Sanctus—and are therefore guardians of the order willed by God. " Before the gods I sing thy praise " (Ps. 137:1).

The next two verses introduce an important corrective, formally pointed out as such by the limiting introductory " nevertheless " and in the content itself by the phrase " in the Lord." Whatever may be the custom of different peoples, in Christ and in the Church the two sexes not only have equal rights but are destined to be much more, each to the other. Each has an immeasurable amount to thank the other for.

THE APPEAL TO NATURAL SENSIBILITY (11:13–15)

[13]Judge for yourselves; is it proper for a woman to pray to God with her head uncovered? [14]Does not nature itself teach you that for a man to wear long hair is degrading to him, [15]but if a woman has long hair, it is her pride? For her hair is given to her for a covering.

Once again Paul appeals to the instinctive feeling for what is proper. " Propriety is binding but it is not the same in all countries and at all times " (O. Karrer). Is it not worth noting that Greek art prefers to show the male body unclothed, but never the female? This shows us still today what was held to be fitting in ancient Greece. Paul may also have thought that the woman who came forward in the communal assembly in this way would draw yet more attention than usual to herself, and that it would be especially inappropriate precisely in this situa-tion, were her physical appearance to evoke increased attention. Paul would like at any rate to strengthen and keep alert natural sensitivity, because it forms a good guide to what is proper and a protection for more essential things. So he does not shrink from strengthening this appeal by bringing in a concept of popular Stoic philosophy much in use in our time but not in the time of the New Testament—nature as teacher.

REGARD FOR CHURCH TRADITION (11:16)

[16]If anyone is disposed to be contentious, we recognize no other practice, nor do the churches of God.

Paul seems himself to calculate that he will by no means convince everyone with his arguments. But in this matter endless
discussion leads to nothing. One can always find something more
to say against each and every thing. But somewhere there must
be a decision, even if it is not understood by all. In this case Paul
sees the decision as given by the common practice of the churches
at that time. (The expression " the churches of God " in the
plural is quite unusual. No doubt Paul wanted originally simply
to point to the multiplicity of churches, meaning communities,
but then attached the qualifying addition " of God " for the sake
of emphasis.) It should be instructive to everyone that in such
matters not everyone, man or woman, can do as he pleases. In a
family it is not possible for everyone to live as he pleases. Nor is
it in the Church of God. Paul's thought or, more precisely, his
concept of the Church is universal through and through. Therefore the passage finishes as it began, with Paul pointing to tradition which comprises not only dogmatic teachings but also dis-
ciplinary matters.

The Proper Celebration of the Lord's Supper (11:17–34)

THE ABUSES THAT HAVE ARISEN (11:17–22)

[17]*But in the following instructions I do not commend you,
because when you come together it is not for the better but for
the worse.* [18]*For, in the first place, when you assemble as a
church, I hear that there are divisions among you; and I partly
believe it,* [19]*for there must be factions among you in order that
those who are genuine among you may be recognized.* [20]*When
you meet together, it is not the Lord's supper that you eat.* [21]*For
in eating, each one goes ahead with his own meal, and one is*

hungry and another is drunk. ²²*What! Do you not have houses to eat and drink in? Or do you despise the church of God and humiliate those who have nothing? What shall I say to you? Shall I commend you in this? No, I will not.*

There was nothing worse the Apostle could say of the scandals that had become apparent than that he believed he should withdraw the title of " the Lord's supper " from their meetings and celebrations. This title was the oldest name we have for what people later called, and are calling again today to an increasing extent, the eucharist. However this requires a note of reservation so far as the period of this letter is concerned, for the name " the Lord's supper " includes the whole meal, of which the eucharistic act was one part, the fraternal community meal the other. The fraternal meal, too, is in its way a supper of the Lord, it is surrounded by the Lord's presence—or should be. The Apostle's rebuke says in effect that this is no longer the case. People meet, and yet there is no real " meeting," but the external assembly brings it about, or makes it plain, that the community is divided. Probably it was the same groups or cliques who gathered together and set themselves apart from the others that Paul had objected to at the very beginning of his letter.

Verse 21 gives us a more precise idea of how we have to think of the Lord's supper both as it is really meant to be, and as it is here in its degenerate form. It was meant to be a fraternal, festive meal, in the evening of course, as always in antiquity. Everyone made his contribution to it according to his position and means, but in such a way that all could then share together. As at a proper meal, each should have his fill, but there ought to be more to it than this. It was meant to express fraternal unity in Christ and therefore to be filled with his presence.

THE ESTABLISHMENT OF THE LORD'S SUPPER AS THE SOURCE AND NORM FOR THE COMMUNITY CELEBRATION (11:23–25)

[23]For I received from the Lord what I also delivered to you, that the Lord Jesus on the night when he was betrayed took bread, [24]and when he had given thanks, he broke it, and said, " This is my body which is for you. Do this in remembrance of me." [25]In the same way also the cup, after supper, saying, " This cup is the new covenant in my blood. Do this, as often as you drink it, in remembrance of me."

After Paul has pronounced the most severe condemnation of the Corinthians' ceremonial meals, he now wants to show in a positive way in what manner, sense and spirit such affairs should take place. For this he must be able to invoke the founder of the Lord's supper himself. He need only recall the precise wording of the sacramental liturgy as it was known to the Corinthians and recited at every celebration. All the rest he will draw from this. The words of Jesus and the action they point to do in fact contain everything.

" On the night when he was betrayed." The oldest ritual formula, like the Roman Canon of today, regarded as important the exact origin of this institution, its circumstances and time, just as the creed also, at the central point of the passion, for the same reason fastened on to the name of Pontius Pilate. The Christian worship, which the Church is to celebrate as long as she herself endures, has an exact historical reference, the same that we call simply " the last supper." The reference to the night, however, also involves a symbolic meaning. This dreadful night in which so much of man's weakness and wickedness was revealed, became the origin of a divine action by which all that is dark has, fundamentally, already been conquered. Over all the dark nights that were to break in upon Jesus' disciples shines already the mystery of victory.

This night is here more exactly described as the one " when he was betrayed." This is more expressive than " when he suffered," although the content of the " suffering " is ultimately the same. Perhaps the translation " given up " expresses this better than " betrayed "—both are possible—because the reference to the fate of the Suffering Servant of God is included. Jesus himself illustrated the death to which he was destined by pointing to this figure—all the more should the Christian community do so. Paul quotes only the formula, but he is hoping that the Corinthians will note the contrast to their own behavior which consisted in everyone taking for himself what he liked.

" Took bread, and when he had given thanks, he broke it, and said . . .": The words are here very ritualistic, stereotyped as in a rubric. For Jesus is carrying out the external action of an Old Testament ceremonial. This is important for an understanding of the " giving thanks." According to its meaning in its origin in Jewish ritual, this is the blessing at meals that does not break down into asking before and thanking afterwards, but in thanking God for his gifts brings about blessing from God. Thanking and blessing were one and the same thing. The breaking of the flat bread took place in order to give each participant in the meal a share in it. Here too one seems to detect the Apostle's wish that the Corinthians should grasp how badly this compared with their own behavior, which was precisely that of not giving.

" This is my body which is for you." These words break through the ritual. They are Jesus' very own. As distinct from the form of consecration entrusted to us in the Roman eucharistic prayer, the words " for you " are here related to the bread, but not linked to it by a verb (" given up "). Even so it is clear what Jesus means by it. It is the body that will be given for them unto death—soon in the frightful spectacle of the cross, and now under the hidden sign of the bread broken for eating.

" Do this in remembrance of me." We are surprised to find the command to repeat the supper here, immediately after the words spoken over the bread. Our liturgy has this command only once (like Luke), after the words spoken over the cup, at the conclusion of the whole eucharistic action. One might ask which is to be regarded as the more primitive form. Has Paul duplicated the command, was it already duplicated in the tradition given to him, or did Luke simplify it? The question is not so important as it may seem to some. Perhaps one observation takes us to the heart of the matter.

" The cup is the new covenant in my blood." " This is my blood " would formally correspond more exactly to the words over the bread, but there are difficulties in all constructions that begin in this way but are also intended to express the idea of covenant. The Pauline construction has made the covenant, the new covenant, the chief predicate of the sentence, but in the other constructions, blood and covenant are closely tied together by the sense, in one way or another. All four versions thereby recall the making of the covenant at Sinai (Ex. 24), take up this covenant therefore, and at the same time replace it with the new. Even though not all four renderings explicitly mention the " new " covenant, it is defined as such by the " my " with " this blood."

" As often as you drink it ": this insertion falls outside the parallel with the first " repetition " command over the bread. Is it perhaps to be explained as an insertion by Paul because he wanted to join something on to it afterwards? The Roman liturgy has taken it over, but did not want to relate it only to drinking but to the whole action. So it has replaced " drink " by " do "—do this, as often as you do this . . . But as is liable to happen in such combinations, the idea is complicated by it and almost obscured.

THE MORAL CONSEQUENCES THAT FOLLOW FROM THIS (11:26-29)

[26]*For as often as you eat this bread and drink the cup, you proclaim the Lord's death until he comes.* [27]*Whoever, therefore, eats the bread or drinks the cup of the Lord in an unworthy manner will be guilty of profaning the body and blood of the Lord.* [28]*Let a man examine himself, and so eat of the bread and drink of the cup.* [29]*For anyone who eats and drinks without discerning the body eats and drinks judgment upon himself.*

To eat this bread, to drink this cup, does not only mean to come into contact with Jesus—that was already said explicitly in 10 : 16. In it there comes about not only the reception of communion, but in this whole act of doing-in-remembrance the death of the Lord becomes in a unique way present, active and effective. Something happens that is handed on further, something objective. Paul calls it " proclaim." It is an announcement of proclamation. The announcement of the gospel can lay claim to being such a proclamation. " Through these words the event that has happened becomes present, that is, reveals its presence, and becomes valid and effective for those present " (H. Schlier). Those present at the eucharistic celebration are the Church, in the concrete the assembled community. In the celebration of the eucharist Christ's saving death attains an ever new power of redemption over the community. For as it " does this " in remembrance of the Lord, he effects in it the salvation contained therein and endows it with the redeeming fruit of his death.

" Until he comes ": this small addition has great significance in many respects. Paul has drawn strongly upon the death of Christ. Bread and wine as sacrificial elements contain it symbolically. The ceremony in which this bread is broken and the cup is drunk is related to the night of the death. Now, however, he has to show the other side as well. What is ever newly given in the bread and wine is the living Christ, the exalted one, who will show forth his life and his power in glory when he comes. The celebration of the Lord's supper is suspended between these two poles: between the death that once was endured, and the revelation-to-be in power. And it has something of both. Much as Paul has to underline for the enthusiastic Corinthians the remembrance of death, he may not and will not underplay the aspect of glory. There is as well another reason why he must include it, especially for the Corinthians. They feel themselves already kings (4:8); they are in danger of overlooking the " not yet." This is partly the reason for the festive mood carried to the point of riotousness of their communal meals. This " until he comes " is a reminder that the kingdom of glory has not yet come.

With this Paul now comes to the practical and critical point at which he has been aiming from the beginning with his reminder of the eucharistic teaching to make the community aware of the contradiction between their conduct and what the Lord's supper really is. His verdict, plainly spoken, is that it is unworthy. This expression has received very precise exposition in Catholic sacramental teaching. It may not be unreservedly applied here, although it is from here that the expression is derived.

" Unworthy " here means, in the first place, something more general: unsuitable. There is a participation in this meal that is unsuitable to its content. This unsuitability becomes sinful because here the body and blood of the Lord are given in a quite definite sense and spirit and must be received in the same spirit. The man who does not want to incur this guilt must reflect whether he really wants to do what he is doing. Whoever examines himself thus attains the required attitude: he may, he should, communicate. But whoever neglects this task of self-criticism does not escape the judgment. He as it were draws it upon himself with this very food, as when someone has taken poison which is not straightaway deadly but is nevertheless an accomplished fact.

But according to what measure should the man, the Christian called to participate in the Lord's supper within the Church, examine himself? Should he go through the ten commandments each time? It is clear from the context from where and about what this self-examination should take place—from Christ and in relation to the community of brethren. Am I ready to take up what Jesus has done for us and makes newly present in what we do together, to make it effective in us? Am I ready to subordinate my own wishes to the just requirements of others? Am I ready to impose renunciation on myself so that more room can be made for love in the world? For what is the use of beating one's breast and what is the use of bowing the knee before the body of the Lord present in the bread, if I despise the body of the Lord which is equally present in the community and especially in its lesser members, if I pass them by to go on to the day's business because for me they are not worth making trouble for myself on their account? The unspecified reference to " body " (11:29) surely means the eucharistic body of the Lord, but it does not exclude the possibility that it can also at the same time mean the body of Christ which is the community. The Corinthians did not recognize it in the poor and humble, nor in those members of the community who held to a different pastor.

THE CONSEQUENCES OF DISREGARD (11:30–32)

[30]*That is why many of you are weak and ill, and some have died.* [31]*But if we judged ourselves truly, we should not be judged.* [32]*But when we are judged by the Lord, we are chastened so that we may not be condemned along with the world.*

We are not a little surprised that the Apostle sees here such a direct relation between the " unworthy communion " of many people, and such physical facts. Jesus' healing of the sick man most certainly had to do with the kingdom of God that he proclaimed. And it was not merely in passing that he gave his disciples the gift of healing to take on their way. And does it not give us cause for thought how often in the closing prayers of the Roman liturgy prayers are offered explicitly for soul and body? In this lies not only evidence of the faith of a bygone age but an offer to those who will grasp it in faith. Certainly we can make no assessment in the particular case. If quite special marvels form part of the missionary situation of a primitive Christian community, then such cases would also form a part of it, as their negative aspect, and be intended by God and pointed out by the Apostles as examples. Naturally in Corinth not all, or only, those were ill or had died who had been guilty in the manner he had condemned, else he would have been able to dispense with his admonition.

Perhaps this nuance is contained in the words of verse 31, " But if we judged ourselves truly," and made plain in the state of affairs just referred to, namely, that not only has each individual to judge himself, but that this judgment can and should also take place in a corporate, united manner within the community. As in the sick and the dead, the sins of the living can be made manifest, so the members of the community should teach and correct each other in good time. When they set one another right in true responsibility and love, one for the other, they spare one another the stricter judgment of God. Paul indeed rebuked them severely for having omitted such a corrective action (5 : 1–8). They may well remember this now.

IMMEDIATE PRACTICAL INJUNCTION (11:33–34)

[33]*So then, my brethren, when you come together to eat, wait for one another—*[34]*if anyone is hungry, let him eat at home—lest you come together to be condemned. About the other things I will give directions when I come.*

Now there is a sudden shift at the close of all these reflections and arguments. They were necessary to show up bad conduct and make recognizable from its innermost center the proper attitude to the celebration of the Lord's supper. But now the point at issue can be most briefly dealt with—" wait for one another." It is true that Paul began this chapter with this point, putting them to shame with his description of their haste, as if some of them were starving. To such people he now says simply and straightforwardly, they should eat their fill at home. The meaning of the Lord's supper demands a true coming together. We meet this expression on two other occasions, and waiting for one another is part of it. That is the dimension of the Lord's supper which they had so basically and painfully disregarded.

The Significance of Charismata for the Church (12:1—14:40)

The Spirit (the *pneuma*) in the biblical revelation is the gift of the end of the ages and the principle of the new creation. We say " the Spirit " and not " the Holy Spirit." This is a preliminary clearing of the way to the reality of spirit in the New Testament. We may not everywhere equate spirit with the third divine Person, although all that is said of the spirit has to do with him. This goes together with the whole history of revelation and salvation.

The Variety of Spiritual Gifts in the Church (12:1–31)

THE MAN WHO SPEAKS WITH GOD'S SPIRIT IS RECOGNIZED FIRST AND FOREMOST BY HIS PROFESSION OF JESUS (12:1–3)

¹Now concerning spiritual gifts, brethren, I do not want you to be uninformed. ²You know that when you were heathen, you were led astray to dumb idols, however you may have been moved. ³Therefore I want you to understand that no one speaking by the Spirit of God ever says " Jesus be cursed! " and no one can say " Jesus is Lord " except by the Holy Spirit.

The way that Paul again immediately broaches this new, great theme shows clearly that he is dealing with an inquiry. He covers the whole range of gifts of the Spirit, but only goes more exactly into those that occur during divine worship, so that this subject too remains in the larger context of the liturgy of the primitive Church, which began at chapter 11. What the Apostle puts forward to start with is intended to make a clear distinction from events with which the Corinthians were familiar from their pagan past. The pagan religious, especially the mystery cults, contained an excess of ecstatic, enthusiastic, even orgiastic phenomena. The idols were indeed, as the Old Testament often said, " dumb," but the demons take advantage of the cult of idols nevertheless, in order to lead people astray. What was coercive, unfree, unworthy of human beings in the pagan cults became very prominent. In the Christian assembly a man was not " transported," he remained completely master of himself. He was not delivered over to inscrutable powers.

We may feel alienated by the curse form which Paul uses as a distinguishing mark, but something of the kind must have happened. The " anathema " form of curse comes from Jewish legal usage. Perhaps it indicates here what Saul the persecutor had himself often uttered in raging hatred, just as in the preceding verse pagan manifestations were touched on. Opposed to both is the profession " Jesus is Lord," the basic and original Christian profession. When the two statements are opposed in this way, each explains the other. " Anathema Jesus ": this is the shortest and strongest expression for a total separation from the person named, even stronger than the words of Peter's denial: " I know not the man," that is, I do not want to have anything to do with this man, as God is my witness. " Jesus is Lord ": this expression is the shortest and the one most packed with meaning for a total bond with him, such a bond as is possible only with God and for him who for me stands in place of God, because God himself has given him for this. I must not be afraid that in this way I take something from God but I should rather be certain that I am affirming precisely what God himself has done for his honor and my salvation.

Before Paul takes into consideration the conspicuous and somewhat extraordinary workings of the Holy Spirit, he established as the most important work of the Spirit simple faith in Christ. This is what he underlines in the negative formulation: " No one can say . . . except by the Holy Spirit."

THE GIFTS OF THE SPIRIT ARE MANY; THE SPIRIT HIMSELF IS ONE AND THE SAME (12:4-11)

⁴Now there are varieties of gifts, but the same Spirit; ⁵and there are varieties of service, but the same Lord; ⁶and there are varieties of working, but it is the same God who inspires them all in every one.

After it has been set out in advance how all expressions of the Holy Spirit are to be distinguished from demonic influences, the Apostle comes to the concrete faults of the situation in the life of the Corinthian community, which was first and foremost characterized by an almost bewildering variety. He understands the basis of this variety: such a springtime of abundance corresponds to the upsurge of the divine life that from now on is to develop within humanity, in the first place in that community of Jesus Christ which opened itself to its influx. Paul underlines only one thing, that all this fullness flows from a single source.

⁷To each is given the manifestation of the Spirit for the common good. ⁸To one is given through the Spirit the utterance of wis-

dom, and to another the utterance of knowledge according to the same Spirit, [9]to another faith by the same Spirit, to another gifts of healing by the one Spirit, [10]to another the working of miracles, to another prophecy, to another the ability to distinguish between spirits, to another various kinds of tongues, to another the interpretation of tongues. [11]All these are inspired by one and the same Spirit, who apportions to each one individually as he wills.

If we at once ask ourselves what can be meant by these categories individually or in what changed form and under what other names they may perhaps be met with today, let us all the same first accept what Paul says about what for him is urgent and important—all these expressions of the Spirit are aimed exclusively at the spiritual benefit of the community. That is the point that concerns him. He mentions it here for the first time. He could not put it off any longer. It is to be repeatedly emphasized with the introduction of each new point. Here lay the basic mistake that the Corinthians had hitherto been making over the gifts of the Spirit. They had seen or sought in them their own gain or pleasure or fame.

Secondly, it is striking what great stress he puts upon their allocation—one to this man, another to that, to no man all of them and to no man what perhaps he would have preferred, but rather what the Spirit holds proper for him in view of the whole. The Spirit wills variety, but a variety that is ordered and thus unifying and enriching. The Spirit is a " Spirit of the whole." This was far from obvious to the pagans—quite the reverse. For them it was quite possible that not only phenomena but also the powers underlying them contradicted one another, just as in their myths the gods struggled with one another. It is not so with the God who " inspires them all in every one " and apportions to each one as he wills. There is a principle of unity in the Church that does not rest in any man's hand and cannot be contained in any human law but lies solely in this Spirit by which God wills to be with his Church and in all the manifestations worked by him.

Nine gifts of the Spirit are listed, without this necessarily being a complete list. Paul repeats three times that the Spirit is their single source. So there can be no rivalry between these gifts. Perhaps the nine manifestations of the Spirit can be divided into three groups. It is difficult to mark them all off clearly from each other, but on the whole it is plain that the entire series is to be understood as a descending one, since it is not by chance that at the end stands the " interpretation of tongues "! There are two at the head : the " utterance of wisdom " and the " utterance of knowledge," these two probably being also ranked in the same descending order of significance. Wisdom may share in the profound vision of God's plans of salvation, even though all that it may know and express leads to worshipful silence before God's unfathomable dispensations. Of this type is the example of the utterance of wisdom that Paul himself offers us concerning the interaction of Israel's destiny with that of the Gentiles (Rom. 9—11). " Utterance of knowledge " is named in second place, perhaps also with the words " according to the same Spirit " somewhat less directly derived from him than utterance of wisdom " through the Spirit," so that the powers of the human intellect come more strongly into play, though at the same time they become better fitted, through the Spirit, to their supernatural object.

If " faith " here appears as a special gift of grace, one must assume that it is a special faith, perhaps that which Paul describes in the next chapter as able to remove mountains (13 : 2). At any rate, it must here be understood as something that has more to do with the building up of the Church than with the salvation of the individual. Probably such faith, which may have become effective through powerful prayer, lies close to the following image.

ANALOGY OF THE BODY AND ITS MEMBERS (12:12-26)

12For just as the body is one and has many members, and all the members of the body, though many, are one body, so it is with Christ. 13For by one Spirit we were all baptized into one body— Jews or Greeks, slaves or free—and all were made to drink of one Spirit. 14For the body does not consist of one member but of many. 15If the foot should say, " Because I am not a hand, I do not belong to the body," that would not make it any less a part of the body. 16And if the ear should say, " Because I am not an eye, I do not belong to the body," that would not make it any less a part of the body. 17If the whole body were an eye, where would be the hearing? If the whole body were an ear, where would be the sense of smell? 18But as it is, God arranged the organs in the body, each one of them, as he chose. 19If all were a single organ, where would the body be? 20As it is, there are many parts, yet one body. 21The eye cannot say to the hand, " I have no need of you," nor again the head to the feet, " I have no need of you." 22On the contrary, the parts of the body which seem to be weaker are indispensable, 23and those parts of the body which we think less honorable we invest with the greater honor, and our unpresentable parts are treated with greater modesty, 24which our more presentable parts do not require. But God has so adjusted the body, giving the greater honor to the *inferior part, ²⁵that there may be no discord in the body, but that the members may have the same care for one another. ²⁶If one member suffers, all suffer together; if one member is honored, all rejoice together.*

The necessity and the perfection too of the unity in diversity and diversity in unity already pointed out, Paul now illustrates by an image—that of the oneness of the body in its many members. He is not the originator of this famous and much used image. It occurs in many places in ancient literature (Xenophon, Livy, Cicero, Marcus Aurelius, Epicurus). As distinct from all these applications, Paul is concerned not with the natural organization of a state, in which citizens should stand together in the common interest, but with an order of grace. The great reality in which all the functions find their unity, from which ultimately they spring, into which they can be integrated, is the Church. Paul does not use the word here (only in 12:28). At the point where he wants to pass from image to reality he says " So it is with Christ " (12:12). He should actually have first said that the Church too is a body. But she is not just any body. She is the body of Christ and so, simply, Christ.

In this passage Paul offers as a basis only one sentence, that of verse 13, a very important one to be sure, which is inserted before the exposition of the image. He bases the oneness of the body on the oneness of the Spirit, and this he bases on the sacramental initiation which was at the same time a sacramental incorporation. Irrespective of whether the two expressions " baptized " and " made to drink " are taken to relate only to baptism, or to baptism and eucharist together (we are of the first opinion), the decisive point is that the sacraments not only bring grace to each recipient but also incorporate him into the oneness of the Church. The Church does not arise afterwards, when the baptized are joined together, but the other way around. The Christian faithful become members of Christ as they have received the one spirit, become one body. The one spirit and one body belong together as much of necessity as soul and body on the one hand, Christ and the spirit on the other. We should note that the word " we " in this sentence includes Paul's own experience of becoming a Christian. By contrast with the original Apostles he had been baptized (Acts 9 : 18).

ITS APPLICATION TO THE BODY OF CHRIST (12:27–31)

[27]*Now you are the body of Christ and individually members of it.* [28]*And God has appointed in the church first apostles, second prophets, third teachers, then workers of miracles, then healers, helpers, administrators, speakers in various kinds of tongues.* [29]*Are all apostles? Are all prophets? Are all teachers? Do all work miracles?* [30]*Do all possess gifts of healing? Do all speak with tongues? Do all interpret?* [31]*But earnestly desire the higher gifts. And I will show you a still more excellent way.*

Whereas at the beginning of the passage of imagery there was an immediate reference to the body—" so it is with Christ " (12 : 12)—now it is put more explicitly—" You are the body of Christ." In connection with what has gone before one may almost understand the sentence as " if you live your membership!" And yet it is certainly right for the sentence to stand without qualification, inasmuch as God has called the community together and has built the body. But the way Paul now specifies the individual members and their functions is very surprising. Quite different names make their appearance, particularly those emphatically placed at the head, again in three precisely calculated gradations : —" apostles," " prophets," " teachers." The absolute basic leading offices of the Church are unmistakable. Here the word " Church " is used deliberately for it is not so certain that each community had an apostle at hand at all times. Besides, it corresponds to Paul's habit and intention to impress it upon the Corinthians particularly that there existed communities in addition to themselves, and that therefore something like the Church stood over them, that they are not in any case the whole Church and not themselves alone the Church. These three divisions, which here appear to be almost as firmly established in verbal usage as other traditions, must represent the basic structure of the communities founded by Paul. Despite the triple form, it is quite different from that which was later established in the Church of bishops, priests, and deacons.

" Apostles " were the founders of the community. They need not have been among the Twelve. This name applied on occasion also to men like Barnabas, Silas, and Apollos. " Prophets " are inspired by the Spirit, they utter the word of God with full authority, in particular situations and to particular people. In the later letter to the Ephesians they also appear together with the Apostles as the " foundation " of the Church (Eph. 2 : 20). " Teachers " had to carry out ordinary instruction in matters of faith—we could say catechesis, introductions to scripture. All three stand in the service of the word, its proclamation. Thus in other lists " evangelists " can also be named, next to " pastors " (Eph. 4 : 11).

The Highest of All Gifts and Most Important of All Virtues: Love
(13:1–13)

The chapter to which we have now to turn our attention has long been specially known as a hymn of praise to love. These thirteen verses bear comparison with the finest passages of world literature, although the author did not aim at anything of the kind. All that justifies such a description in terms of its outward form is strengthened by the relative unity and self-sufficiency of its theme. But it would also be a mistake to doubt its appropriateness in this context. High as the Apostle carries his vision of love in this part of his dictated letter, and however much his words are winged thereby, there is not a line in which he has overlooked the occasion and purpose of correcting the Corinthians' scale of values. He seems to speak of himself personally: "If I . . ." He seems to speak of love in itself: "Love is . . ." But each statement touches on a weak or wounded place among his readers.

WITHOUT LOVE ALL THINGS, EVEN THE BEST, ARE NOTHING (13:1–3)

¹*If I speak in the tongues of men and of angels, but have not love, I am a noisy gong or a clanging cymbal.* ²*And if I have prophetic powers, and understand all mysteries and all knowledge, and if I have all faith, so as to remove mountains, but have not love, I am nothing.* ³*If I give away all I have, and if I deliver my body to be burned, but have not love, I gain nothing.*

Three "if" sentences make up the formal scaffolding of the first verse. They are not unreal sentences, quite arbitrarily constructed. They are quite straightforwardly constructed—" If I speak . . . but have not . . ." Paul really does have many of the gifts he brings in here. To be sure, he exaggerates them yet further. He wants to go to the extreme, because even then what he wants to say still remains true, and indeed it comes out all the more strongly what love is as compared with all that. All the gifts and marvels listed are great, but they must bow to the ground before love.

Not only the heart but the voice too of the man filled by God, seized by the Spirit, must overflow. At any rate, those seized by the *pneuma* in those times tried to express the inexpressible, or to sing out, to draw from word and breath, the highest that speech can offer. But the man thus carried away in speaking can also very much express *himself*. He could, in bringing his whole personality into play, do more to please himself than to help others. To be witness of ecstatic happenings could make others falsely curious or envious. Of its nature and in God's sight such a speaking could be empty and hollow.

In essence the same applies also to charisms, which the Apostle places higher as such than " speaking in tongues." " Prophetic powers " do not only refer to foretelling the future, but as inspired utterances are also an uncovering of the hidden things of the heart, to arouse and comfort. " Understanding all mysteries " refers less to new revelations than to the understanding of their relationships. From there the Apostle moves on to another aspect of faith in which he speaks, following Jesus' words (Mat. 17 : 20) of being able to " move mountains." But even such a faith, confirmed by miracles, would be nothing without love. If to us it may seem unthinkable that anyone should have such faith and be void of love, let us learn from the sermon on the mount that one can cast out devils in the name of Jesus and yet be one of those he knows not (Mat. 7:23).

But where great works of love are done, and not only great but really the greatest, there love must surely be? Yes and no! Certainly love will do these things, but they are not yet an unfailing proof of true love. Where it is a question of such outright heroic acts of love, it is hard indeed to imagine the simultaneous absence of love. This then is the critical point. But we can know from our own experience that even in such circumstances when a man seems and means to give himself up totally to his fellow men, he can still be pleasing himself. The frightful thing is that it is possible to move away from love through works of charity.

LOVE ITSELF BRINGS FORTH ALL THAT IS GOOD IN SUPER-ABUNDANCE (13:4–7)

⁴Love is patient and kind; love is not jealous or boastful; ⁵it is not arrogant or rude. Love does not insist on its own way; it is not irritable or resentful; ⁶it does not rejoice at wrong, but rejoices in the right. ⁷Love bears all things, believes all things, hopes all things, endures all things.

" Love is . . .": how does the Apostle know? Has he simply assembled here ideal characteristics? By no means. He has a picture before him from which he is reading them off. More precisely there are two pictures, one positive and one negative. The positive picture is the existence of Jesus Christ, in which the love of God has revealed itself in human form. The negative picture is the behavior of the Corinthian community. The definitions of love that follow can be understood, point by point, from these two pictures.

That the behavior described here is extremely uncommon is especially confirmed by the fact that a large part of the description is put in the negative—eight times it says what love does not do. This can only be related to the fact that the positive expressions simply described what people were naturally like and how they ordinarily behaved. If things are to go differently, then a powerful force is needed to make a man be able to swim, as it were against the stream. In all this there comes through particularly clearly what the Apostle sees in the Corinthians.

The four last phrases are of a quite different kind. Fortunately, it is not sufficient to speak of love only in negatives. For it is the most positive thing there is, and that in all its aspects. Love fulfills every possibility and every opening for good. Hence comes this triumphant fourfold " all things." Were it not love of which this is said, then it would be a miscalculation from within, or an excessive demand from without. Only love can be so rich in all that follows from it that it does not at once become exhausted by it, as every human being would otherwise be.

ONLY LOVE IS ALREADY NOW WHAT IT CAN BE FOR ETERNITY (13:8–13)

8Love never ends; as for prophecies, they will pass away; as for tongues, they will cease; as for knowledge, it will pass away. 9For our knowledge is imperfect, and our prophecy is imperfect; 10but when the perfect comes, the imperfect will pass away. 11When I was a child, I spoke like a child, I thought like a child, I reasoned like a child; when I became a man, I gave up childish ways. 12For now we see in a mirror dimly, but then face to face. Now I know in part; then I shall understand fully, even as I have been fully understood. [13]*So faith, hope, love abide, these three; but the greatest of these is love.*

What could possibly be said of love, after such great things have been said of it? What has been said can be summed up in the phrase—he who does not have love, has nothing; he who has love, has everything. But this " everything " is not yet exhausted. So far love has been described, not exclusively but primarily, in temporal terms. Patience presupposes conditions of life in which it can break down. Jealousy arises where one is afraid of losing or partly losing the beloved. If love is not resentful, this is to recognize at any rate that wrongs exist. And to endure all things is only possible where such endurance is hard. Is love then bound to the forms of this world? Can love only be practiced, or at least display all its greatness, only against the background of an unredeemed world? And then, does it fall away with the completion of redemption, with the transformation of the world? The man who has love has eternal life. It is precisely the man who has love thus engaged within time who has what endures beyond all time—very differently from those powers or gifts which look much more as if they already possessed a share in the divine and eternal life.

No one can begin other than as a child, but no one should wish to remain at this stage. Childhood must be grown out of, it must be taken up into the more mature stage. Is not the Apostle here trying to tell the Corinthians that their attitude and the value judgments lying at the base of their behavior have something immature about them?

And is it not the same with faith? Sometimes it is light to us, and another time we feel abandoned, alone with oppressive riddles, as in a mountain landscape which at one moment is visible before us in bright sunshine, so that we can see our way forward and behind, and the next moment is so wrapped in mist that a traveler can no longer know his way in either direction. Paul, however, does not take into consideration here such extreme expressions, although he is the author of the contrast: " We walk by faith, not by sight " (2 Cor. 5 : 7). He says only: " We see in a mirror." We use a mirror when we cannot see directly (to look at oneself is not meant here). This mirror technique can be great art, but it is still only a substitute, particularly as the mirror of those days did not possess the technical perfection of today and was not without distortions and blind spots. In these circumstances the observer has to try to complete the picture correctly, but seeing then comes close to guessing. It does not have the certainty that leaves no question open. In every transmission or mediation irreplaceable nuances are lost or can only be laboriously pieced together.

" Face to face ": this is what we hunger for among ourselves, and hunger for particularly with God. For what we have already been able to experience of immediacy among men, what has already been able to give us happiness, we cannot yet have experienced with God. This is only possible " then." Paul even chooses for us the active form of knowing which he avoided in 8 : 3. Indeed, he goes very far in the interchangeability of the mutual knowing by God and man. This interchangeability can certainly not be intended to set God and men on the same level, but being known and knowing can obviously be closely related to one another, so that the knowing corresponds to the being known, so far as this is humanly possible.

From that " then," from the time that is to be, the Apostle brings our attention back again. Now it is a matter of faith, hope, and love. These are in any case more important than

speaking in tongues, prophesying, and possessing deep knowledge. These three in essence already transcend the imperfect.
They have already a more direct access to God, an immediate
sharing in God. They are, in all the simplicity that pertains to
the believer, divine virtues—so related to God that men can
only practice them by God's grace or, to put it the other way
round, so given by God that through them man has a share
in God's self-disclosure.

*Directions Appropriate to All the Circumstances Concerning the
Spiritual Gifts of Speaking in Tongues and of Prophesying
(14:1–40)*

WHY PROPHECY DESERVES TO TAKE PRECEDENCE OVER SPEAKING IN TONGUES (14:1–25)

*[1]Make love your aim, and earnestly desire the spiritual gifts,
especially that you may prophesy. [2]For one who speaks in a
tongue speaks not to men but to God; for no one understands
him, but he utters mysteries in the Spirit. [3]On the other hand,
he who prophesies speaks to men for their upbuilding and
encouragement and consolation. [4]He who speaks in a tongue
edifies himself, but he who prophesies edifies the church. [5]Now
I want you all to speak in tongues, but even more to prophesy.
He who prophesies is greater than he who speaks in tongues,
unless some one interprets, so that the church may be edified.*

Even after expounding so brilliantly the highest standard of
value, love, the Apostle cannot dispense with the examination
of details. It was the same with the question of sacrificial food.

He showed them his pastoral shrewdness and love. He knew how hard people found it to draw conclusions that in themselves are clear and logical, where these run counter to their inclinations. So Paul seeks to do everything in his power to win the Corinthians over to the practical details he thinks right and necessary. He by no means dispenses with reflection and example when these can serve his purpose—hence the very varied arguments, working on different levels, in order to convince everyone so far as possible. By good fortune we can also discover in this text something more precise about these two gifts of the Spirit.

The man speaking in tongues speaks on behalf of God, speaks mysteriously, edifies himself. This is not bad in itself, but others gain nothing from it. The man who speaks with inspiration speaks to others and they receive edification, admonition, and comfort thereby. So one sees that such prophesying or speaking from inspiration can be something not so far removed from what preaching and spiritual exhortation attempts, here of course effectively attained by characteristic power. For speaking in tongues we cannot find anything so easily comparable. It is the expression of ecstatic transport or emotion in which, however, it escapes any testing of its genuineness by others. There was, of course, also the possibility of the speaker in tongues repeating later in comprehensible speech what he had said earlier in a state of ecstasy. The Apostle would not put any restriction upon this since he was not fundamentally opposed to speaking in tongues as such.

⁶Now, brethren, if I come to you speaking in tongues, how shall I benefit you unless I bring you some revelation or knowledge or prophecy or teaching? ⁷If even lifeless instruments, such as the flute or the harp, do not give distinct notes, how will any-

one know what is played? [8]*And if the bugle gives an indistinct sound, who will get ready for battle?* [9]*So with yourselves; if you in a tongue utter speech that is not intelligible, how will anyone know what is said? For you will be speaking into the air.* [10]*There are doubtless different languages in the world, and none is without meaning;* [11]*but if I do not know the meaning of the language, I shall be a foreigner to the speaker and the speaker a foreigner to me.* [12]*So with yourselves; since you are eager for manifestations of the Spirit, strive to excel in building up the church.*

Paul again points to his own example. If he were to give free rein to his own speaking in tongues, what would the community he was visiting gain from it? It is important for us to learn in this connection what he means to bring with him on his pastoral visits—" revelations," " knowledge," " prophecy," " teaching." These four do not give the impression of a systematic order, nor are they exhaustive. But they are examples of what the community might expect from him in real gain. The example taken from musical instruments is revealing insofar as utterances spoken in tongues also have something musical about them, but were comparable to a music whose content could not be understood. May one think here of modern forms of music whose place in worship is affirmed by some, contested by others? We can leave it to the future to decide what in these forms will assert itself as a genuine liturgical expression. But certainly singing in the liturgy is the form of expression which could and should best arouse the sort of enthusiasm which in those days was realized in speaking in tongues. That applies to singing as a whole, but it applies particularly to the style of the singing.

After these examples Paul returns to the matter itself, to the

" language " of the speakers in tongues. If they speak a totally incomprehensible language, they are really " speaking into the air," or, to put it somewhat less drastically, they are speaking totally over people's heads, as if they were among people who spoke an unknown foreign language. For them the cultivated Greek used the word " barbarian," by which he did not so much mean lack of culture as try to imitate the incomprehensible sounds of a foreign language. Thus Paul is touching a little upon national pride when he explains to the Corinthians that in their speaking in tongues they are really behaving like barbarians.

[13]*Therefore, he who speaks in a tongue should pray for the power to interpret.* [14]*For if I pray in a tongue, my spirit prays but my mind is unfruitful.* [15]*What am I to do? I will pray with the spirit and I will pray with the mind also; I will sing with the spirit and I will sing with the mind also.* [16]*Otherwise, if you bless with the spirit, how can anyone in the position of an outsider say the "Amen" to your thanksgiving when he does not know what you are saying?* [17]*For you may give thanks well enough, but the other man is not edified.* [18]*I thank God that I speak in tongues more than you all;* [19]*nevertheless, in church I would rather speak five words with my mind, in order to instruct others, than ten thousand words in a tongue.*

What should a man do who has the gift of speaking in tongues? He need not deny it or neglect it. He should pray for the " power of interpretation " (by himself or by another). At the root of all these explanations, guidances, and admonitions lies the certainty that even in relation to these extraordinary endowments of the Spirit a man is by no means purely passive, let alone unfree. Again and again it has to be said that the Corinthians brought such notions with them from the pagan cults. But they do not correspond to what the Holy Spirit brings about in the man in a state of grace. He does not wish to unleash uncontrollable powers of unreason. When Paul distinguishes in speaking with tongues which he here—and only here—equates with prayer, between " praying with the spirit " and " praying with the mind," " spirit " here means that power or area of the human being which is raised above and beyond itself in inspiration, while " mind " is more or less equated with consciousness. Higher though the possibilities of the spirit (*pneuma*) of man may be than his consciousness, the combined operation of both is nevertheless needed if genuine results are to be gained.

Paul concludes this liturgical reflection with the strongest possible emphasis. In the assembled Church he would rather speak five words that mean something to others than ten thousand ecstatic words in a tongue.

[20]*Brethren, do not be children in your thinking; be babes in evil, but in thinking be mature.* [21]*In the law it is written, " By men of strange tongues and by the lips of foreigners I will speak to this people, and even then they will not listen to me, says the Lord."* [22]*Thus, tongues are a sign not for believers but for unbelievers, while prophecy is not for unbelievers but for believers.* [23]*If, therefore, the whole church assembles and all speak in tongues, and outsiders or unbelievers enter, will they not say that you are mad?* [24]*But if all prophesy, and an unbeliever or outsider enters, he is convicted by all, he is called to account by all,* [25]*the secrets of his heart are disclosed; and so, falling on his face, he will worship God and declare that God is really among you.*

For the third time in this letter the Corinthians are told that in their whole behavior they are lagging behind at a childhood stage. There is indeed a true spiritual childhood in which consists the perfection that Jesus called for (Mat. 18:3) and Peter praised (1 Pet. 2:2), but here it is a question of a lack of that judgment that is necessary for an adult and mature person.

Paul takes a further argument from Isaiah. There is a passage in this prophet (Is. 28:11) where God threatens his people with " men of strange tongues " and with " the lips of foreigners." (Because this echoes a verse from Deuteronomy [28:49], it can be said to be " in the law ".) That meant at the time that the Assyrians would occupy the land. Paul is able to use this saying here to emphasize to the Corinthians that " strange tongues " are not always a sign of God's graciousness or nearness. It is in any case true that believers receive more from inspired speech which they can understand, whereas speaking in tongues may make more of an impression on the uninitiated.

PRACTICAL CONSEQUENCES (14:26-40)

²⁶*What then, brethren? When you come together, each one has a hymn, a lesson, a revelation, a tongue, or an interpretation. Let all things be done for edification.* ²⁷*If any speak in a tongue, let there be only two or at most three, and each in turn; and let one interpret.* ²⁸*But if there is no one to interpret, let each of them keep silence in church and speak to himself and to God.* ²⁹*Let two or three prophets speak, and let the others weigh what is said.* ³⁰*If a revelation is made to another sitting by, let the first be silent.* ³¹*For you can all prophesy one by one, so that all may learn and all be encouraged;* ³²*and the spirits of the prophets are*

subject to prophets. [33a]*For God is not a God of confusion but of peace.*

The last example Paul has applied quite closely to the situation he has to regulate. The spiritual wealth of the community (1:5) should take full effect in the liturgical assembly. All should take their proper place, within the limits and according to the order that assures the objective of edification, as against its opposite. What a picture of a vital community and its liturgy! " Each one has . . ."; this of course presupposes a still relatively small community, otherwise the meeting would have been endless. Again the list seems anything but systematic, even less than that of the charismata, some of which take practical effect here.

As for the item named in the second place, " a lesson," we see how highly Paul values it. It was not yet reserved to the official teachers but was also a free gift of the Spirit. It will have consisted largely in the interpretation of scripture. The whole Old Testament had still to be given a Christian interpretation.

"A revelation" must mean the disclosure of concealed connections, which, however, did probably not remain in general terms, as for example the lesson, but touched on something specific.

" A tongue " and its " interpretation " are at first cited only once, in order to bring them within the highest rule, namely, that everything should happen for edification, by which is meant not edification in the narrow sense of a state of mind but the ordering and strengthening of the community in faith. Its background is the image of the building of the Church, which God is building but which at the same time is given over to its members to build with him (cf. 1 Pet. 2:5ff.). Then come particular rulings: of speakers in tongues there should be only two, at most three, and only this many, or any at all, when an interpreter is there. Paul does not accept that a man might be so seized by the Spirit that he could do no other. Rather, he takes for granted that the true spirit shows itself in this submission to proper order. Even the prophets are subject to a similar limitation.

" The spirits of prophets are subject to prophets." The plurality of spirits should not be understood as meaning independent being, neither the Holy Spirit nor other spirits. It means much more those organs in men that come into action under such influence. Such " spirits " can get in each others' way and create confusion just because what is human plays a great part in it, not because God comes so immediately to utterance. What comes from God can only promote unity, peace, and order.

[33b]*As in all the churches of the saints,* [34]*the women should keep silence in the churches. For they are not permitted to speak, but should be subordinate, as even the law says.* [35]*If there is anything they desire to know, let them ask their husbands at home. For it is shameful for a woman to speak in church.*

As if he were making a direct connection with 11:5, and as if he had to anticipate all resistance with this powerful argument, the Apostle demands, invoking the common practice of the Church (the expression "churches of the saints " is quite rare!) that women would keep silence in the assembly. But were we not to understand that he freely allowed them to pray in the assembly and to speak under the inspiration of the Spirit, only not unveiled? This belief may be maintained. If we look into the matter more precisely, he does not forbid women to communicate an inspiration granted them—we have examples of this, such as the four daughters of Philip the Deacon (Acts 21:9), but only to argue about what has been said. The reason for this restriction lies in what the society of that time, in the Jewish as well as the Greek world, held as proper. When Paul invokes the law, i.e. scripture, as well, this is because it was not so familiar to born Greeks as to born Jews, but for Christians should be decisive.

36What! Did the word of God originate with you, or are you the only ones it has reached? 37If anyone thinks that he is a prophet, or spiritual, he should acknowledge that what I am writing to you is a command of the Lord. 38If anyone does not recognize this, he is not recognized. 39So, my brethren, earnestly desire to prophesy, and do not forbid speaking in tongues; 40but all things should be done decently and in order.

Paul has now surely said the last word on this point. One feels in his sentences how great was the inclination of the Corinthians to judge everything from their own point of view and to question everything again and again. Against this Paul established decisively that no one is a Christian for himself alone, so that he has only to judge according to his own insight. Being a Christian is only possible as a member of Christ's body and therefore by integration and subordination. It may be that " in itself " there is always something more that could be said against it, but this cannot come from a good spirit. Paul here commits his whole apostolic authority. The question of where the Apostle takes this " command of the Lord " from is therefore of no consequence. He knows that this, and only this, is according to the mind of the Lord, and he therefore transmits it to the Church.

The man who is not willing to recognize it is not recognized by God.

These strong words, equivalent to the threat of an implied excommunication, the Apostle does not want to be his last on this point. He speaks again to the Corinthians as " brethren," and sums up as briefly as possible the essential content and object of the entire chapter.

THE RESURRECTION OF THE DEAD (15:1-58)

The two major groups of questions to be dealt with are now completed. What had to be said about the clearing up of abuses in the community and in explanation of the relevant moral questions has been said. The inquiries concerning liturgical matters have been answered. One great matter the Apostle has saved till the end. He wants to give it the greatest weight.

Christ's Rising: The Basis and Center of the Gospel (15:1-11)

All Christian Preaching Rests on the Apostolic Tradition (15:1-3a)

[1]*Now I would remind you, brethren, in what terms I preached to you the gospel, which you received, in which you stand, [2]by which you are saved, if you hold it fast—unless you believed in vain.*

[3a]*For I delivered to you as of first importance what I also received . . .*

Right at the beginning our attention is aroused by the fact that Paul does not, as elsewhere in this letter, take up a question put to him but rather introduces the subject of himself. Nevertheless this "reminder" of the gospel does not mean that he wants to tell them something new. It is, he says at once, the gospel "I preached to you." According to the sense it is a forceful reminder of what they have already heard. But because

156

some (many?) have given themselves up to ways of thinking or speaking, to a tendency and mentality that contradicts it, they must hear the message anew, and that all the more carefully because it is the basis of their whole existence as Christians. It should be noted how, on the purely stylistic level, the Apostle emphasizes the completely decisive power of the gospel by a succession of short relative clauses. Only in verse 3b does he come to what he means by the gospel itself.

The man who accepts the gospel is saved, for this is what the good news offers—rescue, salvation (cf. Rom. 1 : 16). This salvation will be revealed in the judgment to come (1 Thess. 1 : 10), but it is already effective in the present, it puts the believer into a definite " state." He is lifted out of the morass of vacillating opinions, fears, or hopes and set upon firm ground, as the psalms often say, or acknowledge with praise. To be a believer in the gospel is the same as to stand in a state of grace (Rom. 5 : 12) —provided, of course, that the gospel is adhered to faithfully. There is in fact a falling away from this state of salvation, a " believing in vain," as the Apostle has observed in a number of ways in the course of the whole letter. The reasons can be various. Here it is abandoning the treasure of faith—which the Church puts before us.

But where is the *Church* mentioned here? The Church is most precisely spoken of at the beginning and end of the chain, at the two ends upon which depends, according to the Apostle's meaning, what is contained in the center—salvation. It is most clearly contained in the two unmistakably corresponding expressions: " I delivered to you " and " What I also received "— that is, what was also delivered to me. Much as Paul can invoke the fact that he himself has seen the Lord—as we shall see shortly—he knows equally that he is an apostolic witness in common with the other witnesses and recognizes that it is specially important for the Corinthians in particular not to look on the Apostle's message and teaching as his own personal property but as the message and teaching of the apostolic Church (15:7, 8, 14). If a community that is full of charismatic life needs to be held and hold itself firmly to the common apostolic tradition, this is more especially true of a community the substance of whose faith is in danger of dissolving by reason of certain individual or fashionable interpretations. The Apostle himself held fast to this tradition, as he here again emphatically assures them.

The Apostolic Tradition Rests on the Official List of Witnesses of the Resurrection (15:3b–8)

. . . *³ᵇthat Christ died for our sins in accordance with the scriptures, ⁴that he was buried, that he was raised on the third day in accordance with the scriptures, ⁵and that he appeared to Cephas, then to the twelve. ⁶Then he appeared to more than five hundred brethren at one time, most of whom are still alive, though some have fallen asleep. ⁷Then he appeared to James, then to all the apostles. ⁸Last of all, as to one untimely born, he appeared also to me.*

As regards the style of this passage we are bound to be struck by the formal repetitions, especially those of a double type. In the first half all the short statements begin with " that." They are therefore dependent clauses. In the second half there are only main sentences: " Then he appeared . . . then . . ." Verse 5 occupies a middle position; it belongs to a certain extent to both types.

This brings us to the next important observation, which contains within itself a whole mass of questions for which we still today have no exact answer. Though it is certain that what Paul cites here are established formulas, it is nevertheless difficult to pin down the precise limits of these formulas. We are deliberately using the plural—formulas. For this much can be said with some certainty—we are dealing here not only with one formulation of faith but with several.

Verse 3b-5 must have comprised the oldest formula. It lists four saving events in Christ: he " died," " was buried," " was raised," " appeared." This corresponds to the core of the apostolic confession of faith. In fact what we see here is only an earlier stage in that process of crystallization which doubtless was formed for the same end that the later somewhat more richly developed profession of faith served—to be the profession of those who acknowledged themselves as members of the Church of Christ. Around this center, but also for the sake of it, the formula was expanded: the origin of Christ was set out in the profession of God the Creator and Father, and there was added to it the future that is opened to all by his saving death—resurrection of the body and eternal life.

Here too in our chapter it really comes down to one point—the resurrection of Christ but in such a way that, even should only this be meant, the other saving events must also be named and professed. If for Paul the whole formula is important enough to call to mind here, then it should also be important enough to us to consider it with the greatest care.

It is the whole formula delivered to them which he describes as " of first importance." Thus it must be regarded in its entirety as the heart and center of the gospel, the main point of what Paul delivered to the Corinthian community as he did, of course, to all the other communities founded by him.

" That Christ died for our sins in accordance with the scriptures." In the Greek text too it says here simply " Christ," not as elsewhere " the Christ." One must conclude from this that already in this very early period, to which this text relates, a few years after Christ's death and resurrection, " Christ " was no longer understood as a title, the Messiah, but had become a second name for Jesus. To put it differently, the office and the person had already merged into each other. No one else but Jesus could be the hoped for Messiah. The first thing known of this Christ was that he died—not, surprisingly, that he was crucified. In the later Creed the two statements stand together: crucified, died and was buried. Possibly in primitive Christianity people at first spoke more often simply of Jesus' dying than of the crucifixion.

The addition " in accordance with the scriptures " relates principally to the dying as such, not in the first instance to the " for our sins." For the Messiah's death was the great scandal that could be overcome only from scripture, when it was shown that God had foreseen this, that this was necessary (cf. Luke 24:26). For this reason the accounts of the passion are all at pains to show in various details that the words of scripture have been fulfilled. From there it was only a step further to the recognition that this " for our sins " was anticipated in scripture, in Isaiah 53, according to which the servant of God " bears our sins," " suffers for us," " is punished for our sins " particularly since Jesus himself had expounded this connection at the celebration and institution of the Last Supper: " The blood . . . poured out for many " (Mark 14:24).

" That he was buried." This second statement does not seem so important in itself as the first and the third " died," " was raised." These two are without doubt the necessary complemen-

tary components of the primitive Christological and soterio-
logical profession of faith that makes up the core of our Creed.
The expressions used may vary in detail: crucified-glorified;
laid low-exalted. Behind them lies a twofold structure, which
expresses already the most ancient Christian preaching of the
mystery of salvation, the paschal mystery.

What is the significance of the phrase " was buried "? It
underlines the reality of the death. Only when he is buried is a
dead man, so to speak, finally and definitely cut off from the
realm of the living. So long as he is not yet buried, they are
still concerned with him. The grave signifies the final parting
and farewell. Thus the burial of Jesus is described in detail in all
the four gospels, just as the empty tomb then plays an important
role in the accounts of Easter. Indirectly the significance of the
empty grave is also detectable in the way it is included in the
sacramental and symbolic participation in Jesus' death and rising
in baptism, when the man who has been immersed comes out
from the grace of the water to the newness of life.

" On the third day." Even this element in the apostolic creed
is considered. But it is not so obvious as it may seem to us
with the creed always ringing in our ears. Paul does not mention
the third day anywhere else. The gospels report prophecies of
the passion culminating in the Resurrection on the third day
or after three days, from which we are able to conclude that
this can in no sense be taken to mean three periods of 24 hours
but that fulfillment of these prophecies did happen within as
short a period as this. But why was this timing so important
that it could be included in a brief formula? Surely for a reason
similar to that which brought Pontius Pilate into the creed—it
was intended to establish a datable event in the history of the
world and of time.

" And that he appeared." We are coming to that part of the primitive Christian kerygma which is of the very greatest importance in the present dispute over the proper understanding of the reality of the Resurrection, so we should like to go into it with some thoroughness. According to the wording, what stands here could be translated as " and that he was seen " (by Cephas . . .). But the New Testament writings (and before them already the Septuagint translation of the Old Testament) express thereby with this phrase, above all the becoming visible of supra-terrestrial realities, that can be granted and achieved by God alone. But it by no means applies to " visions," by which we mean inner experiences in which the person affected " sees " something which has no reality outside himself. Many such visions have occurred in the history of revelation, above all with the prophets, who for that reason were called " seers." Paul too knew such visions, which we reckon as mystical phenomena. He speaks of " visions and revelations of the Lord " (2 Cor. 12 : 1–4) but distinguishes these very precisely from the seeing of the risen Christ. Only with reluctance will he abandon anything of that experience. With this " having seen " he ranges himself with the official witnesses whose testimony is an obligatory foundation of faith for the whole Church.

". . . to Cephas, then to the twelve." Only here, in this document, is the appearance of Jesus to Peter cited as of such first importance, as so basic. Probably it is the same that is mentioned in the story of Emmaus, where the disciple who had stayed in Jerusalem said to those who were returning: " The Lord has risen indeed and has appeared to Simon " (Lk. 24 : 34). Clearly the reference to Simon by the Aramaic name Cephas is also an indication that in the primitive Church the task of being the foundation, which Jesus laid upon Peter when he gave him this name, was known and stressed. For it is not so completely certain that this appearance was the first in time as that it was considered to be the first in rank. Probably, of course, both are meant here.

After the head, the " collegium " is cited. Paul does not use the expression " the twelve " elsewhere. The official character of this number is stressed by this appearance, all the more in that it would not be of great importance if at that point in time the number had been only eleven.

" Then he appeared to more than five hundred brethren at one time, most of whom are still alive, though some have fallen asleep." In the language and rhythm a new element can clearly be seen here. The statements with " that," in the dependent form, are abandoned and Paul goes on in main sentences. What corresponds to the original formula—" that " statements or main sentences? This question is not easy to decide, for there are examples of each. Probably Paul has linked several formulas together without hesitating to make additions. The statements about most being still alive while some had fallen asleep would be difficult to fit into a formula. We are bound to be struck by the large number, even if one takes into account that in biblical writings large numbers are not of the same exactitude as smaller, and that the man of antiquity had something of the same attitude to them as do children today who are all at sea when it comes to distinguishing between amounts that exceed their power of measurement. In any case this appearance cannot have occurred in the very first Easter days, since it presupposed a community of disciples already grown to respectable size. One may not include any women among them, because here it is only the official list of witnesses that is supposed to be given. If the large number has something suspicious about it, this suspicion is disarmed by the reference to the fact that these witnesses are still alive and can be encountered and sought out.

"Then he appeared to James, then to all the apostles." This sentence, with its two parts, closely resembles verse 5. James, the "brother of the Lord," held or was increasingly coming to hold a leading position in Jerusalem, second only to Cephas. At the Council of the Apostles it was these two who led the controversy and brought it to a decision.

But who are "all the apostles"? Probably not only the twelve. The concept of apostle can also be taken in the wider sense, in which case, of course, it cannot be said exactly how many it means. But in the circle within which the formula was coined, people would certainly have had an exact idea about it.

"Last of all, as to one untimely born, he appeared also to me." This sentence comes unmistakably entirely from Paul himself, but it is nevertheless quite deliberately attached to the preceding chain of witnesses. This is surprising because we are accustomed to thinking of the Easter appearance as closed with the Ascension or at any rate not as extending over years, as is necessary in this case. But the appearance to more than five hundred brethren already requires us to go beyond the Ascension. Luke's portrayal, on which our idea of the forty days concluded by the Ascension rests, need not be regarded as the only possible one.

The List of Witnesses Is Completed by Paul (15:9–11)

⁹For I am the least of the apostles, unfit to be called an apostle, because I persecuted the Church of God. ¹⁰But by the grace of God I am what I am, and his grace towards me was not in vain. On the contrary, I worked harder than any of them, though it was not I, but the grace of God, which is with me. [11]*Whether then it was I or they, so we preach and so you believed.*

Paul can never forget, wants never to forget, that he had persecuted the Church, that he was an enemy who hated God's loving and salvific will—God who already possessed in the Church a body on earth. But whether or not he is worth it and worthy of it—he has now become an apostle and knows that he, alone and much more than others, has to thank the freely given grace of God for this. And because he owes to it his being an apostle, so too he owes all the fruits of his apostolic service. He can already, although he is still in the midst of his apostolic course, declare in all objectivity that he has worked and achieved more than the others. This assertion does not dispense with grace, and conversely the presence of grace does not dispense with the efforts of the Apostle. Grace does not remove the power of what is personal, the human being in all his individuality. He knows that all is grace and wants to give honor to grace, but there is still no need to ignore the fact that grace has been capable of this " with him," with his readiness, with all the spiritual capabilities that he had by nature and had obtained through education, and with the passionate gratitude with which since that day he acknowledged his debt to the Lord.

Our Resurrection Stands and Falls with the Resurrection of Christ (15:12–19)

The Resurrection is Indivisible (15:12–13)

[12]*Now if Christ is preached as raised from the dead, how can*

some of you say that there is no resurrection of the dead? [13]*But if there is no resurrection of the dead, then Christ has not been raised.*

Only now do we discover what was the occasion for the Apostle to demonstrate so forcefully the basis of belief in the Resurrection —some people say that there is no Resurrection. Basically this is too little for us to be clear about the intellectual origins and context of this erroneous opinion or dangerous tendency. It does not seem to have been, as yet, a formal denial of the Church teaching, nor a rejection of it, or it would not have been possible for the Apostle to address them all as " brethren." On the other hand he must on the whole have regarded the tendency which he summarizes as very dangerous because he deals with it in such detail. These people probably did not simply deny the Resurrection of Christ but rather interpreted it in a sense which, in the Apostle's judgment, came to the same in its result as denying it.

Our Faith Stands and Falls with Christ's Resurrection (15: 14–16)

[14]*If Christ has not been raised, then our preaching is in vain and your faith is in vain.* [15]*We are even found to be misrepresenting God, because we testified of God that he raised Christ, whom he did not raise if it is true that the dead are not raised.* [16]*For if the dead are not raised, then Christ has not been raised.*

These people really do not know what they do when, in one way or another, they interpret either what happened in Christ or what is to happen to all the dead, in a manner that Paul condemns as a falling away from the apostolic preaching and tradition. They are breaking up the faith. They are turning it into a world view, a humanism. Preaching or gospel on the one hand, faith on the other, then become empty words, all the more empty the more they, closely examined, can be traced back to the earthly standards of man's common experience of his own nature. Then there is no message from another world and no standpoint outside ourselves.

For those who preach such a message something still worse is implied. They have not only fallen victim to a gross and naïve misunderstanding, but they have thereby borne, false witness on God's behalf. The whole seriousness of the apostolic message, its incomparable claim, become apparent here—the apostles' total absorption in the knowledge that they are directing this message to the world in God's name. Certainly they have much else to say and to teach, but it all has value insofar as this message is true. " Easter is the security for all Christian teaching " (W. Meyer). What would be the authority of Christ which Paul invokes from the beginning to the end of the letter? What would be the apostolic office? What would be this whole Christian reality to which Paul repeatedly refers himself and the community? What would be meant by the phrase " in Christ "? What would be the celebration of the Lord's supper, what would be his body, if it were the body of a dead man?

Our Entire Hope Rests on Christ's Resurrection (15:17–19)

[17]*If Christ has not been raised, your faith is futile and you are still in your sins.* [18]*Then those also who have fallen asleep in Christ have perished.* [19]*If for this life only we have hoped in Christ, we are of all men most to be pitied.*

A new argument should make the whole position clear to the waverers who did not yet perceive the consequences of their weakened understanding of the faith. If there is no real, bodily resurrection, then faith—and all that is done according to the mind of faith—is in vain, wasted effort. " You are still in your sins." For Paul there is an indissoluble connection between sin and death. Death is not only the punishment consequent upon sin, but its completed expression. It cannot be avoided by postulating an immortal part of man. It is not enough to save the soul. Salvation is indivisible, man is indivisible. This does not mean in practice that the forgiveness of sins happens only on the last day. But it means that the forgiveness happening now has already something to do with the resurrection. By it we become already a new creation (2 Cor. 5 : 17).

That we must still die does not mean any essential break. We are already " in Christ." We go into it in him, and on the other side we are already " with " him—thus Paul is to express it later (Phil. 1 : 23). But if Christ is not risen, if the new creation is not begun in him, what happens to us then? Paul can point out to the Corinthians certain cases of death that must have recently occurred in their community. What help would it be to them that they had " fallen asleep in Christ "? They would be lost in that dark realm of death in which separation from God prevails.

And those still living, what would it mean for them, how far would it take them? Paul seems to be saying that for himself, he would in that case do something better than spend himself in the service of this message and this faith. With this idea he wants to bring into play a theme that can ultimately be illuminating for everyone but was bound to frighten Christians who were dealing in notions and interpretations that sooner or later give rise to such consequences.

The Totality of the Resurrection Seen in the Light of Saving History (15:20–28)

The Principle of Resurrection (15:20–22)

20But in fact Christ has been raised from the dead, the first fruits of those who have fallen asleep. 21For as by a man came death, by a man has come also the resurrection of the dead. 22For as in Adam all die, so also in Christ shall all be made alive.

With this liberating, indeed triumphant " But in fact " Paul turns away from his long negative argument (" If . . . ") to a positive presentation and development of the certainty of salvation. He shows the whole history of the world and its salvation illuminated by the light of resurrection. The perfect tense of the verb in the first half of the sentence established once more, in the form of a profession of faith, what has happened and what its effects are. Christ is and remains raised up, risen. What is added to it in the form of a simple apposition, " the first fruits of those who have fallen asleep," contains already all the consequences that Paul uncovers in what follows.

This connection, the total structure of saving history, which lies at the base of this line of thought and gives it its stringency, is made clear by the Apostle when he compares it with the oneness of humanity in Adam (cf. 5:12, 21), where St. Paul points out that we are all subject to sin and death. He sees here an all-embracing parallel, which of course God has freely established, between man's oneness in the fall, which derives from Adam, and the oneness in salvation which exists in Christ. This oneness in the fall could be recognized as such only in the light of the oneness in salvation. Only thus could the categories appropriate to the oneness of salvation be applied analogously to the link with Adam, not only the " by " but also the " in."

The Stages of Resurrection (15:23-24)

23But each in his own order: Christ the first fruits, then at his coming those who belong to Christ. 24Then comes the end, when he delivers the kingdom to God the Father after destroying every rule and every authority and power.

Parallel as verses 21 and 22 were, so that one explains the other, and slight as the difference can be between " by " and " in," it is still worth noticing that verse 21, in the Greek, has no verb —only the principle is stated—whereas in verse 22 there are two verbs—one in the present, " all die," and one in the future, " shall all be made alive." The best explanation of this is that the false teachers of Corinth interpreted the resurrection as only spiritual and existential and thus as having already happened. Paul had to emphasize the fact that something decisive was still to happen and thus also to elucidate the meaning of its fulfill-ment in time. This happens in the following verses which define a little more precisely what is meant by the concept " first fruits of those who have fallen asleep." He now takes up this concept again. There is an order as much in time as in importance. In each respect the first place belongs to Christ.

In the second place, as the second limb, is the position of all who belong to Christ by faith and baptism. Certainly Paul, when he wrote this, did not reckon on such a long interval between the Resurrection and the Second Coming, but that changes nothing essential in the circumstances. It has, however, rightly been asked whether what is meant here is a process in two or three stages : (1) Christ, (2) the Christians, (3) the others, the rest. The insertion " each " certainly leads one to reckon on only one more stage. But on closer examination one must settle for two stages all the same, at any rate as far as time is concerned (particularly as the meaning " the rest " cannot be given to the word *telos,* the end).

The Final Completion (15:25 28)

[25]*For he must reign until he has put all his enemies under his feet.* [26]*The last enemy to be destroyed is death.* [27]*"For God has put all things in subjection under his feet." But when it says, "All things are put in subjection under him," it is plain that he is excepted who put all things under him.* [28]*When all things are subjected to him, then the Son himself will also be subjected to him who put all things under him, that God may be everything to everyone.*

While in verse 24 the to a certain degree military, political note that sounded in the expression " rank " or " order " had been intensified (" rule," " authority "), now this image becomes yet more comprehensive. We find the idea of the subjection of the enemy no less than six times. " He must reign." Here a theology of the kingdom of Christ is developed, and at the same time something like a theology of history. Thus the " end " (15:24) and the delivering over of the kingdom are taken up still more explicitly. Time has a goal. Progress should be possible within it. Little as the period of the Apostles and the New Testament writings was affected by any idea of progress, this verse can stand as important support for it.

Human Considerations (15:29–34)

The "Baptism on Behalf of the Dead" (15:29)

²⁹*Otherwise, what do people mean by being baptized on behalf of the dead? If the dead are not raised at all, why are people baptized on their behalf?*

In this passage a couple of palpable facts are assembled, depending less on strict logic than on their dramatic effect. In the first place there is the curious practice of so-called vicarious baptism—a person had himself baptized on behalf of a deceased relation or friend. Though such a custom is unknown to us, it ought not to strike us as totally incomprehensible. Do we not do something similar with Masses and indulgences when we apply them to the dead, and with everything that one does for the dead, partly in ways recognized by the Church, partly out of pious feeling? It corresponds to a general human need to be able still to do something for the dead. In relation to baptism early councils strictly forbade this practice while some sects continued it. Paul here neither approved nor condemned it. It is sufficient for him to make use of this practice to argue that it has sense only if Christ's resurrection can still have an effect on the dead. In

order to see the strictness of this prohibition and the openness
to other practices in the proper relationship to one another, one
may say that for those who are in Christ the possibility of
believers acting as representatives for and among each other is
almost boundless, and that the Church does not lightly set limits
upon love that ventures so much. She had, however, in those
centuries at any rate, to protect the sacraments from magical
abuses.

The Apostle's Life Expounded (15:30–32a)

[30]*Why am I in peril every hour?* [31]*I protest, brethren, by my
pride in you which I have in Christ Jesus our Lord, I die every
day!* [32a]*What do I gain if, humanly speaking, I fought wild
beasts at Ephesus?*

More actual is the example that Paul illustrates in himself, by
his life as an apostle that brings him continually to the verge
of death. Why should he take the heavy burden of this life upon
himself if there were no resurrection of the dead? One sees that
for the Apostle the idea of the immortality of the soul does not
exist. The division, so familiar to us, according to which the
soul can exist separated from the body, means nothing to him.
Here our modern understanding of ourselves is again slowly
approaching the biblical idea, though we naturally do not wish
simply to abandon the gain that the concept of the soul, taken
from the Greek thinkers, has brought us. To what experiences
in Ephesus Paul is referring has not been explained to this day.
The expression for " fighting with beasts " that Paul uses here
belongs to the technical vocabulary of the amphitheatre.

A Collection of Pressing Motives and Palpable Warnings
(15:32b–34)

³²ᵇ*If the dead are not raised, "Let us eat and drink, for tomorrow we die." ³³Do not be deceived: "Bad company ruins good morals." ³⁴Come to your right mind, and sin no more. For some have no knowledge of God. I say this to your shame.*

This brings Paul on to proverbial expressions and he adds one that seems to have belonged to the store of school education in antiquity. It comes from a comedy by Menander. But the warning with which the Apostle goes on is directed less towards the heathen than to such " brethren " who endangered, by their weakened faith, the faith of others as well.

But what is the meaning of the abruptly inserted injunction to come to their right mind? Who is drunk or out of their senses here? This injunction in particular is evidence that the whole argument has been occasioned by a spiritualistic interpretation of the Resurrection which was supported by the phenomena of enthusiasm and thus transcended time. Because these people felt they had already reached perfection by overrating their " knowledge " (*gnosis*), Paul now tells them sharply that some have no knowledge of God.

The Nature of the Risen Body (15:35–44a)

Illustrated by the Analogy of the Transformation of Seed-Corn
(15:35–38)

³⁵*But someone will ask, " How are the dead raised? With what*

kind of body do they come?" [36]*You foolish man! What you sow does not come to life unless it dies.* [37]*And what you sow is not the body which is to be, but a bare kernel, perhaps of wheat or of some other grain.* [38]*But God gives it a body as he has chosen, and to each kind of seed its own body.*

The image of sowing was much used at that time as is shown by several of Jesus' parables (the most closely related in content is John 12:24). While Jesus' sayings are set with prophetic economy and give hints rather than exposition, Paul displays his pastoral love and his stylistic skill alike in the way he now brings out more clearly the three points of the comparison: the starting point—the sowing of the bare seed; the objective—the emergence of a new body; and between these two the decisive point—the dying. Does not everyone know it, even if he does not have to care for field or garden? It is always a matter of the new thing we hope for, but precisely for the sake of this new reality, the old must first go into the earth and thus into the mystery of dying.

" But God gives it a body as he has chosen." We would say without reflection that Paul is taking a comparison from nature, and indeed we can certainly also say that nature brings this about, even if we are inclined to call it a miracle every time, especially when the Resurrection in new bodily form unfolds before our eyes in spring. Our scientific thinking is arrested by this grandeur that we call nature. But if the spiritual man at least can still marvel at this event that goes on so much more quietly and yet with so much greater power than all his most powerful " creations," this is yet another reason to follow the Apostle's thought—which, in accordance with the whole thought of the Bible, sees God at work in natural forces, and not only in concentrated, streamlined forces such as man too can set to work

but infinitely varied, bringing forth the inexhaustible variety
of forms and species—to each of the seeds its own body.

*Expounded by Comparison with the Many Forms and Levels of
Life and Living Bodies (15:39–41)*

[39]*For not all flesh is alike, but there is one kind for men,
another for animals, another for birds, and another for fish.*
[40]*There are celestial bodies and there are terrestrial bodies; but
the glory of the celestial is one, and the glory of the terrestrial
is another. [41]There is one glory of the sun, and another glory of
the moon, and another glory of the stars; for star differs from
star in glory.*

Paul now develops and illuminates the idea or rather the image
of each creature with its own body, so as to make the new kind
of risen bodily existence more nearly accessible to wavering
human thought. He opens up the picture book of the visible
creation for man and shows him the forms of life that surround
him. He changes from the expression " body " to " flesh."
" Flesh " means the whole manner of appearance and, of course,
existence too, which binds man to the beasts in common conditions. And yet, how many are the differences, the adaptation and
beauty of the fishes in all their kinds, birds in all their kinds,
land animals in all their kinds, and finally men. Paul does not
otherwise use many words for this positive view of nature, but
much of it is contained in this verse and context.

Then he turns up another page of the picture book, for which
he goes back to the expression " body," which in this case can be
rendered by the expression " celestial bodies " and " terrestrial

bodies," to which he refers in the next two verses. Again one cannot fail to notice that for good or ill Paul acknowledges a certain " glory " in the terrestrial bodies also. For what is due to the celestial is also proper for the earthly, though the latter glory may lie at a far lower level than the former.

Celebrated in a Short Antiphonal Hymn (15:42-44a)

[42]So it is with the resurrection of the dead. What is sown is perishable, what is raised is imperishable. [43]It is sown in dishonor, it is raised in glory. It is sown in weakness, it is raised in power. [44a]It is sown a physical body, it is raised a spiritual body.

It now appears how, in what has gone before, it was not the differences as such that were important but solely the illustration of the boundless creative power of God, which is always able to go further, so that every level points to a yet greater marvel. With his " So it is " is answered, too, the whole question that dominates this section, the " how " of the Resurrection, by referring to God's creative power to which nothing is impossible, and which indeed shows forth its greater glory precisely where it seemed to have been lost. There now follows a short hymn, singing antithetically of these wonders. The basic fact of death is described four times in forms familiar to us, so as to contrast it anew with the ever more transcendent glory of the Resurrection body. There is a corresponding opposition in each pair. The redemption corresponds to the creation, but it heals its wounds and transcends it. Between this first and that second creation lies the inescapable fate of death, but this dying has become, through Christ, the beginning of transformation, of glory. What creation began redemption will complete. What death threatens to snatch away is raised up by Christ's resurrection in yet greater hope, to be completed on his "Day" in bodily glory.

A Survey from the Last Things to the First, and the First Things to the Last (15:44b–58)

The First Adam and the Last (15:44b–49)

[44b]*If there is a physical body, there is also a spiritual body.* [45]*Thus it is written, " The first man Adam became a living being "; the last Adam became a life-giving spirit.* [46]*But it is not the spiritual which is first but the physical, and then the spiritual.* [47]*The first man was from earth, a man of dust; the second is from heaven.* [48]*As was the man of dust, so are those who are of the dust; and as is the man of heaven, so are those who are of heaven.* [49]*Just as we have borne the image of the man of dust, we shall also bear the image of the man of heaven.*

We have here an example of what Paul calls " the wisdom of God in the Spirit ": " The unspiritual man does not receive the gifts of the Spirit of God, for they are folly to him, and he is not able to understand them because they are spiritually discerned " (2:14). Certainly if we only had our visible world of experience we could not conclude from it compellingly that there must also be a glorified world, a bodily existence through which spirit could do yet more than through our present world. But since we know through Christ of the existence of that higher creation, not only can we accept the fact in faith but we can also recognize its " logic," its fittingness, its correspondence, for the mysteries of faith illuminate each other, as the First Vatican Council said.

Paul grants us straightway an insight into the source of this higher knowledge. It is the illumination of the account of creation by and in relation to Christ. A sentence in the second creation story has become important to him—" and man became a living being." The Old Testament author wanted to say in his own way that man, formed out of the " dust from the ground," had received a vital principle from God. One may call it " soul " if one does not mean by this simply and solely a metaphysical, spiritual, and therefore immortal substance. For this concept did not lie within the range of the biblical author's speech and thought. According to the principle that Paul applies far-reachingly to Adam and to Christ, both elements in this description are now related to Christ, and both are thereby intensified. Christ is animated not only by that transitory life, the *psyche,* but also by an immortal soul or spirit. Indeed he himself is the principle that can transmit this spirit, this life-giving *pneuma,* to the whole of creation. In him begins the new creation. He is the second Adam—Paul says the " last Adam," because there can be only one corresponding to the first. There is only one act that equals the creation, includes and supersedes it—the new creation in Christ. Paul is so convinced of the strictness of his own logic of revelation that he does not even spell out clearly the transition from the citation from Genesis to his conclusion.

With Jesus begins a new humanity. If one would ask exactly where this beginning lies, with the Incarnation or with the Resurrection, the answer is not easy. On the one side, for Paul, the spiritual reality of Jesus only " broke through " in the Resurrection, but that does not exclude this spiritual reality's presence in the Incarnation. What Jesus was in himself since his Incarnation will in any case only become communicable after his exaltation (cf. Rom. 1:4).

The All-Embracing Transformation (15:50–53)

[50]*I tell you this, brethren: flesh and blood cannot inherit the kingdom of God, nor does the perishable inherit the imperishable.* [51]*Lo! I tell you a mystery. We shall not all sleep, but we shall all be changed,* [52]*in a moment, in the twinkling of an eye, at the last trumpet. For the trumpet will sound, and the dead will be raised imperishable, and we shall be changed.* [53]*For this perishable nature must put on the imperishable, and this mortal nature must put on immortality.*

Closely as Paul showed the connection between belonging to Christ and the glory of the Resurrection in order to impress upon those who denied the Resurrection their lack of logic, he has equally to stress on the other side that between our present position as Christians and that glorified bodily existence, there is a barrier to be surmounted—so as not to end up by giving impetus to the same error, that they have already thought to have surmounted. The expression " flesh and blood " in itself means nothing other than the natural, physical body, but what is perishable in it is now emphasized. Jesus himself left this " flesh and blood " behind him on the Cross and in the grave.

But in what does the " mystery," so solemnly proclaimed, consist? It cannot be in the fact that some will experience the *parousia.* Nor in the fact that those apocalyptic events will break upon us so suddenly and amid such phenomena, for all these aspects contribute to the general value of his presentation of the last things (cf. 1 Thess. 4:16; Mt. 24:31). Nor can Paul have

meant by it that he together with some of those now living would
be present then, though of course he certainly reckoned on this.
The mystery must lie in the transformation that all, one way
or another, will experience.

With the prospect of this " change " Paul gives his answer to
the question that might, indeed must, arise when he proclaims
so emphatically that " flesh and blood cannot inherit the kingdom "—are not those who live to experience the *parousia* straightway excluded? The grasp of this " change " to a certain degree
surpasses or replaces death. For those affected it will be as pain-
less as putting on a new garment.

The Expected Song of Victory (15: 54–57)

[54]*When the perishable put on the imperishable, and the mortal
put on immortality, then shall come to pass the saying that is
written: " Death is swallowed up in victory."* [55]*" O death, where
is thy victory? O death, where is thy sting?"* [56]*The sting of
death is sin, and the power of sin is the law.* [57]*But thanks be to
God, who gives us the victory through our Lord Jesus Christ.*

If then some are snatched back from death and others transported
into a new existence in a way unimaginable to us, all in fact
undergo a transformation. Jesus said on one occasion: " No one
can enter a strong man's house and plunder his goods, unless
he first binds the strong man " (Mk. 3: 27). Something like this
happened sporadically, symptomatically, with the casting out of
demons. This victory will be completed on the day the " last
enemy " is destroyed. This is how death is seen—personified.
That is why Paul now gives voice to a kind of song of victory,
with elements from the prophets. The words here are a com-

bination from Isaiah 25:8 and Osee 13:14. Apparently this quotation was brought in by the word for " swallowed up," by which the most comprehensive and radical strains contained in " putting on " are continued and perfected. To " swallow up " means that all the old reality completely disappears. Till now the jaws of death had in a way swallowed up everything —now death will itself be swallowed up. The man who lives through " that day " will look around and see no trace anywhere of what now extends everywhere over the earth. Paul and the man who believes with him can already, in faith, anticipate this vision and taste this triumph in advance (cf. 2 Cor. 5:17). The " sting " may mean the goad used for a herd of oxen, or it may be the poisonous sting of the scorpion. The sting of death is in any case an image which in the Apostle's mind is at once filled with ideas essential to his preaching. Verse 56 reads like a summary of his exposition in the letter to the Romans concerning the power of sin (Rom. 6 and 7). But he does not stop with his song of victory. It is only—in musical terms—an introduction. While everything seems already to be pressing forward to the end, the counterpoint appears again. But its purpose is only to make all the more liberating the experience of a resolution of all struggle in a radiant victory.

The Present Consolation (15:58)

58Therefore, my beloved brethren, be steadfast, immovable, always abounding in the work of the Lord, knowing that in the Lord your labor is not in vain.

To praise God in this way for the work of salvation is right and proper. But neither should we leave out the other element that is appropriate to our present position. Paul prefers to end the chapter not with triumphal notes but with warm yet urgent warnings. He speaks again to his " brethren," as at the beginning of the long chapter. Now he adds the word " beloved." He would like to assume that he has won back the waverers to the full unity of faith and now begs and warns them to be steadfast and not let themselves again be led astray, so that they can devote themselves with undivided strength to the building up of the community and the spreading of the gospel.

OFFICIAL AND PERSONAL MATTERS: INSIGHTS INTO THE BEGINNINGS OF THE WORLD-WIDE LIFE OF THE PRIMITIVE CHURCH (16:1–18)

The main questions have been answered, the great dogmatic themes that were thrown up have been exhausted. To that extent this chapter is only an epilogue. And yet it is significant for us. Do our communities live only by the great themes of preaching? Do not quite concrete tasks, affairs and personal relations play a considerable role? We may be astonished that even such things form part of the holy scripture. But how important this very knowledge is. In it is implicitly recognized that such things not only exist and are to continue, but that they are allowed to exist in God's sight. Besides, these remarks are a further stamp of authenticity. No one indeed doubts that this letter originates with Paul. But even if someone else had been capable of composing such a letter, who would have troubled to invent this information about his movements, these references to this and that?

The Levy for Jerusalem (16:1–4)

¹*Now concerning the contribution for the saints: as I directed the churches of Galatia, so you also are to do. ²On the first day of every week, each of you is to put something aside and store it up,*

as he may prosper, so that contributions need not be made when I come. ³And when I arrive, I will send those whom you accredit by letter to carry your gift to Jerusalem. ⁴If it seems advisable that I should go also, they will accompany me.

This collection is to be made " for the saints." This means, as verse 3 clearly says, the community at " Jerusalem." Even if all the communities are " churches of the saints " (14 : 33), they are so only as offshoots or additions to the original Church (cf. Eph. 2 : 11–22). The awareness of owing the faith to this mother Church was very much cultivated in the early Church.

In many respects it was shrewd to arrange that this collection should be brought to Jerusalem by members of the Corinthian community. People would make quite special efforts to collect a proper amount. Still more vital connections would be forged by personal acquaintance. Above all, it would avoid the appearance of being a personal interest of Paul's. The urgency with which Paul again takes the matter up in his second letter to the Corinthians (chapters 8 and 9) does not indicate that the initial enthusiasm was great enough. Clearly he no longer expected any effect if he proposed to be present himself. The factional spirit, the individualism, the joy in argument, the spiritual pride, everything that Paul had to combat in Corinth certainly did not form a climate in which generosity for such spending could flourish.

The proposed journey to Jerusalem, that he here mentions for the first time, was to be his last. It led to his arrest.

The Apostle's Immediate Travel Plans (16:5–9)

⁵I will visit you after passing through Macedonia, for I intend to

*pass through Macedonia, *and perhaps I will stay with you or
even spend the winter, so that you may speed me on my journey,
wherever I go. *For I do not want to see you now just in passing;
I hope to spend some time with you, if the Lord permits. *But I
will stay in Ephesus until Pentecost, *for a wide door for effective
work has opened to me, and there are many adversaries.*

Paul includes the community in his missionary plans. Young as
these churches all are, he does not leave them a purely passive,
receptive role. It is a matter of course to him and to them that
they are interested in the spreading of the word of God, the
foundation of the new churches, and the fate of those already
established. They should take part at least by their prayers. The
expression " that you may speed me on my journey " does not
mean a mere letting go but a much more active participation
in the Apostle's next task. But even if they are only to pray,
with proper zeal and perseverance, they must know what is
planned and what is happening. The Apostle shows in various
ways how much they have to reckon with changes—" Perhaps,"
" I hope," " if the Lord permits." He had discovered often
enough that the Lord wanted something different from what
his Apostle had planned (cf. Acts 16:7). That is part of something that an Apostle is no more spared than other men. In fact
Paul stayed in Ephesus for two and a half years altogether, until
the riot unleashed by the silversmith Demetrius which almost
cost the Apostle his life, and put a forcible end to his missionary
activity. The second visit to Corinth announced here also took
place, though delayed. Corinth was to remain a missionary center
until it was replaced by Rome. But how difficult this stay was
the whole second letter to the Corinthians shows in retrospect.

The Journey of the Two Apostolic Representatives (16:10–12)

[10]*When Timothy comes, see that you put him at ease among you, for he is doing the work of the Lord, as I am.* [11]*So let no one despise him. Speed him on his way in peace, that he may return to me; for I am expecting him with the brethren.* [12]*As for our brother Apollos, I strongly urged him to visit you with the other brethren, but it was not at all his will to come now. He will come when he has opportunity.*

The sending of Timothy had already been announced to the community (4:17): " Therefore I sent to you Timothy, my beloved and faithful child in the Lord, to remind you of my ways in Christ." He was almost too young for this mission in a tense situation. If the Corinthians made it difficult for him, he might lose heart. That is why the Apostle identifies himself with him and stands over him in an almost fatherly way.

" He is doing the work of the Lord." Indeed, completely literally it reads—he works the work of the Lord. It is worth paying attention to this expression. In what sense can a man work the work of the Lord? Another passage runs, " Do not, for the sake of food, destroy the work of God " (Rom. 14:20), and here this work of God means the Church, more exactly the unity in faith and love of the Church, which in this letter is called " God's field, God's building " (3:9). That men can be " God's fellow workers " (3:9) in this work is anything but obvious. And yet such work is by no means reserved to Apostles. Paul charges them all: " Be steadfast, immovable, always abounding in the work of the Lord " (15:58). The work of the Lord is thus as much a work for the Lord's cause as it is ultimately the working of the Lord himself. Only he can do this work, but he chooses to do it through the cooperation of those called to the Church.

Final Injunctions (16:13–18)

[13]Be watchful, stand firm in your faith, be courageous, be strong. [14]Let all that you do be done in love. [15]Now, brethren, you know that the household of Stephanas were the first converts in Achaia, and they have devoted themselves to the service of the saints; [16]I urge you to be subject to such men and to every fellow worker and laborer. [17]I rejoice at the coming of Stephanas and Fortunatus and Achaicus, because they have made up for your absence; [18]for they refresh my spirit as well as yours. Give recognition to such men.

It becomes ever clearer that Paul is rapidly nearing the end. In these four successive injunctions one can see attitudes common to and ever repeated in primitive Christianity, but one is also justified in seeing references to the defects that have come to light in this long letter and summaries of the necessary remedies. The injunction to watchfulness is valid for all Christian time, because it is eschatological time. It comes from Jesus and is constantly repeated by the Apostles. It is needed by the Corinthians against everything that threatens to eat away their faith. They are to be or become courageous in order to overcome the childish things that Paul has pointed out to them more than once. Strong they should be in all things in which they were lax and negligent. The injunction to love, which is the most fully expressed of these injunctions, takes up more plainly than the rest what has been said at the beginning against the danger of factions, and at the end against all misplaced charismatics, and concerning the preservation of order, peace and true perfection.

The next two verses are still more concrete and personal. There are three names mentioned, principally that of Stephanas —the other two belonged (perhaps as slaves?) to his " household," of which we know that Paul baptized them all (1 : 16). These three are at present in Ephesus. Were they perhaps the bearers of the Corinthian letter of inquiry, and were they to bring back this answer?

However, their visit seems to have meant far more to the Apostle and perhaps to have lasted longer than would have been needed for an exchange of letters. He found comfort in their presence and the hope that it must go well with a community from which such men came. The household of Stephanas receives the honorary title of " first converts in Achaia " that was a title in various senses of the word. It was used in other churches also, and was to a certain extent granted inasmuch as a definite recognition was expressed from which followed certain consequences. The title does not rest so much upon Stephanas himself being literally the first to be baptized but more on the fact that he at once put his household at the disposal of the mission and the Church growing up around it. Such people were the existing leaders of the churches. The natural authority which he had gained by his " service " to the growing community was acknowledged and reinforced by Paul, saying Yes, the Corinthians should be subject to him, they should listen to him and to every other such " fellow worker and laborer." All this is not yet officially institutionalized, but we are seeing here how this office for the administration of the Church, which is to form the backbone of the Church of the future, is in process of development. It still lies at the margin of the letter. In his letter Paul has discussed the affairs of the community with its whole membership. But we learn once again that personal interventions play a part, and we discover that it is the express will of the Apostle that such men as Stephanas and his two companions be obeyed. He wrote something similar to this to the Church at Thessalonica also (1 Thess. 5 : 12).

THE ENDING OF THE LETTER (16 : 19-24)

¹⁹The churches of Asia send greetings. Aquila and Prisca, together with the church in their house, send you hearty greetings in the Lord. ²⁰All the brethren send geetings. Greet one another with a holy kiss.

²¹I, Paul, write this greeting with my own hand. ²²If anyone has no love for the Lord, let him be accursed. Our Lord, come! ²³The grace of the Lord Jesus be with you. ²⁴My love be with you all in Christ Jesus. Amen.

This letter has already supplied us more than once with proof of how strong the consciousness of the bond between the primitive Christian churches was, and how it was cultivated. It is part of the basic attitude of an emerging church to know that it has been taken up into an all-embracing society, the society of the " Catholic " Church. The greetings testify to this bond.

Aquila and Prisca were especially closely attached to the young Church at Corinth, as can be seen from the Acts (Acts 18 : 1-3). But we meet this couple in Ephesus too, where Apollos first really won them over to the Christian faith and the mission (Acts 18 : 26), and then again in Rome (Rom. 16 : 3). They must have had " houses " or businesses in many cities but they had clearly put their whole fortune and influence everywhere at the service of the gospel.

Up to now Paul has dictated. But it was his custom to write a few words in his own hand as a kind of signature (cf. 2 Thess. 3 : 17; Gal. 6 : 11). This final greeting contains four short sentences. The first is of frightening seriousness, it almost represents a curse. Against whom is this directed? Actually it can only be directed against people who are within the Church but do not bind themselves to the Lord with their whole heart, but rather love themselves, depend on men, engage in personality cults and injure the community. The community should not let itself be guided by such people, hence this curse.

Its positive counterpart is the prayer " Our Lord, come," (*Marana tha*). The two expressions *anathema* and *marana tha* stand opposed to one another as do those of *anathema* Jesus and *kyrios* Jesus (12:3). The expression *marana tha* is left in the Aramaic in the Greek text, like " abba " (Rom. 8:15 and Gal. 4:6), and they are both valuable evidence of the prayer of the primitive Palestinian community which was taken over by the Greek-speaking churches (as today we still have Amen, Alleluia, Hosanna). But why was the " *marana tha* " not kept? In the *Didache* it belonged to the eucharistic liturgy : " May grace come and this world pass away. Hosanna to the Son of David. If a man is holy, let him come. If he is not, let him do penance. *Marana tha*. Amen " (10:6). Likewise the Apocalypse uses it, in Greek of course, as its closing prayer and thus among the last words in the New Testament: " Come, Lord Jesus " (Rev. 22:29). This translation is evidence of the two possible translations, " The Lord comes " or " Our Lord, come." The latter is probably the correct one, and this is probably the reason why this cry was later lost when the Church no longer lived in expectation of the Lord.

" The grace of the Lord Jesus be with you " and " My love be with you all in Christ Jesus " are both liturgical blessings. Even if Paul writes from a distance, he nevertheless keeps the idea of speaking to the community as he would if he were in its midst, where his letter is to be read out.